PIERRE CORNEILLE

by Claude Abraham

Intended for the general reader who does not have the French required to consult the references available in that language, this volume concentrates on the dramatic writing of Corneille. The first chapter gives his literary biography while subsequent chapters treat his plays chronologically so as to show the definite evolution of his dramatic canon. The purpose is to show that Corneille's work is both coherent and monolithic, and to explain why precisely those of his fans who had most avidly cheered him in earlier years were most puzzled by his last masterpieces.

ABOUT THE AUTHOR

Born in 1931, Claude Abraham is professor of French at the University of Florida. He has published extensively (five books, about twenty-five articles), mostly on the literature of seventeenth-century France. His book on the influence of Malherbe won the 1970 SAMLA Studies Award. He is the recipient of numerous study grants, including one from the National Endowment for the Humanities. His professional organizations are AATF (president, Florida, 1971-73); MLA (chairman of French I, Midwest, 1964); SAMLA (chairman of French I, 1969); ACTFL (advisory assembly 1968-69).

SERIES

rature

rsity

nch, Emeritus

i

anguages

TWAYNE'S WORLD AUTHORS SERIES (TWAS)

The purpose of TWAS is to survey the major writers—novelists, dramatists, historians, poets, philosophers, and critics—of the nations of the world. Among the national literatures covered are those of Australia, Canada, China, Eastern Europe, France, Germany, Greece, India, Italy, Japan, Latin America, the Netherlands, New Zealand, Poland, Russia, Scandinavia, Spain, and the African nations, as well as Hebrew, Yiddish, and Latin Classical literatures. This survey is complemented by Twayne's United States Authors Series and English Authors Series.

The intent of each volume in these series is to present a critical-analytical study of the works of the writer; to include biographical and historical material that may be necessary for understanding, appreciation, and critical appraisal of the writer; and to present all material in clear, concise English—but not to vitiate the scholarly content of the work by doing so.

Pierre Corneille

By CLAUDE ABRAHAM
University of Florida

Twayne Publishers, Inc. :: New York

Preface

Seventeenth-century scholars may readily ask whether another book on Corneille is either necessary or desirable. Every year at least one book and countless articles are added to the already overwhelming Cornelian bibliography. Yet, in spite of this deluge, there have been few books in English aimed at the English-speaking nonspecialist. In fact, only two come to mind; one of these, *A Study in Corneille* by Lee D. Lodge, is nearly a century old and is not readily available. The second, *Corneille* by P. J. Yarrow, is a book which, although frequently stimulating, is marred by highly subjective—and often unwarranted—judgments and selectivity. Thus, *Mélite* is discussed at length, but *Le Cid* is dismissed in a few paragraphs. In short, I know of no book aimed at the modern English-speaking general reader, one who would be unwilling to cope with secondary literature in French and whose interests are not so fixed as to warrant the reading of highly specialized theses.

It should go without saying that I make no pretense to any new discoveries or approaches. Basing myself on the work of specialists such as André Stegmann, Robert Nelson, Georges May, Serge Doubrowski, Jean Starobinski, to name but a few of the many to whom I owe an immense debt, I have attempted to write a book that would help the general reader. As a result, I have kept the quotations and the critical apparatus to a minimum. The translations of Corneille are my own, based on the critical editions for the early comedies and on the Marty-Laveaux edition for the rest of his works. These are all listed in the bibliography.

Some readers will deplore the omission of certain topics. It may be argued that to discuss Corneille without treating at length his debt to Spain and to the Italian theater, his involvement with the social and political events of his times, is to ignore important facets of his life and of his work. This cannot be denied, but the scope of this study makes such a total treatment impossible. I have therefore tried, in these few pages, to show the work of a giant, a work that is coherent and monolithic but whose coherance was subject to a profound and steady evolution. The biographical sketch will therefore neglect the usual sequence of daily events for the sake of a more "literary" approach, one which, it is hoped, might better explain why precisely those fans of Corneille who had most avidly cheered him in his early days were most puzzled by his last masterpieces. A chapter on the sociopolitical background would, nevertheless, have been most desirable. I therefore recommend to even the most casual reader of seventeenth-century French literature the perusal of one of the books on this background listed in the bibliography.

CLAUDE ABRAHAM

University of Florida

Contents

Chronology

The plays are listed according to first performances. The dates given in parentheses after the titles are of the first publication.

1606 Birth of Pierre Corneille in Rouen, June 6.

1615 Enters the Jesuit school of Rouen, one of the best in France at the time.

1618 Obtains the first prize in Latin versification, an honor he will duplicate in 1620.

1622 End of the *collège* years and start of law studies.

1624 Passes his bar examinations but because of bad diction pleads only one case. His parents then buy Corneille two magisterial charges whose duties he will conscientiously perform until 1648.

1625 Birth of Thomas Corneille. Pierre will have a lifelong influence on this younger brother, helping him immensely in his education and contributing no little to Thomas' successful dramatic career.

1629 The great actor Montdory forms the theatrical group of the Marais, and it is probably that year that they perform Corneille's first play, *Mélite* (1633). The success of the play contributes no little to that of the entire troupe.

1631 First publication of a work by Corneille, a small liminary poem. *Clitandre* (1632).

1632 *Mélanges poétiques. La Veuve* (1634).

1633 *La Galerie du Palais* (1637).

1634 *La Suivante* (1637) and *La Place Royalle* (1637).

1635 Under the protection of Richelieu five authors, including Corneille, collaborate on *La Comédie des Tuileries*. Corneille is most likely the author of the third act. In England *Mélite* is the first of many foreign successes. *Médée* (1639).

1636 *L'Illusion comique* (1639).

1637 *Le Cid* (1637). Corneille joins the "Five Authors" for a text since lost. His father is granted nobility by the king. The quarrel of *Le Cid* rages. One of the earliest attacks, Scudéry's *Observations sur Le Cid*, prompts Corneille's *Lettre apologétique*, a masterpiece of irony. Late that year the *Sentiments de l'Académie sur Le Cid* are published although Richelieu had ordered a halt to the attacks. *L'Aveugle de Smyrne*, last effort of the "Five," to which Corneille probably wrote the first act.

1640 *Horace* (1641) and *Cinna* (1643).

1641 *Polyeucte* (1643). Corneille marries Marie de Lampérière, also of the upper middle class.

1642[?] *Pompée* (1644) and *Le Menteur* (1644).

1644[?] *La Suite du Menteur* (1645), Corneille's last true comedy.

1644 Publication of the first edition of the collected works (the first eight plays). Candidacy rejected by the Academy probably because he does not live in Paris.

1645 *Théodore* (1646) and *Rodogune* (1647).

1646 Second rejection by the Academy, for the same reasons.

1647 *Héraclius* (1647). Having promised to move to Paris, Corneille is elected to the Academy.

1648 New edition of the collected works (16 plays). These editions now become very frequent.

1649 Corneille and Beys write occasional poetry for Valdor's engravings illustrating *Les Triomphes de Louis le Juste*. *Don Sanche d'Aragon* (1650).

1650 *Andromède* (1651). *Nicomède* [early 1651?] (1651).

1651 Publication of the first twenty chapters of the *Imitation*.

1652 *Pertharite* (1653).

1656 Complete edition of the *Imitation*, a tremendous success (four editions that year alone). Thomas Corneille, who has been guided and protected by his brother, obtains what is perhaps the greatest dramatic success of the century with his *Timocrate*.

1659 *Œdipe* (1659).

1660 Seventh edition of the works. The plays are revised and accompanied by three *Discours* on dramatic poems. *La Toison d'or* (1661).

1662 *Sertorius* (1662).

1663 *Sophonisbe* (1663).

1664   *Othon* (1665).

1666   *Agésilas* (1666).

1667   *Attila* (1667).

1670   *Office de la Sainte Vierge. Tite et Bérénice* (1671).

1671   *Psyché* (1671), the result of the combined efforts of Quinault, Molière, and Corneille.

1672   *Pulchérie* (1673).

1674   *Suréna* (1675). The king revokes Corneille's pension without giving any reasons. It is reinstated in 1682.

1684   After nearly one year in senility, Corneille dies (September 30). His brother Thomas takes his seat at the Academy.

PETRVS CORNELIVS. ROTHOMAGENSIS
Anno Dñi 1643.

PIERRE CORNEILLE

CHAPTER 1

Life

I *Early Years: In Search of a Career*

CONSIDERING the longevity of Corneille and the high
esteem in which he was held by his contemporaries, we
know very little about his private life and even less about his relationship with other members of the republic of letters. Most of
what is generally advanced in those realms is pure conjecture. We
know, for instance, that Rouen, the city of Corneille's birth and
early years, was the publishing capital of French theater in the
early years of the seventeenth century and that there were fairly
large Spanish and English colonies there, but we know nothing
concerning Corneille's involvement with any of these. Careful
reading of Corneille's works leads to many logical surmises but to
few unquestionable facts.

That little is known of Corneille's private life need not distress
us, for its effect on the work of the author seems to have been
minimal. It would be very rash, for example, to suggest that the
plays of Corneille are the result of his social or ethnic origin.
Pierre Corneille shared much of his routine with his younger
brother Thomas; yet they had little in common in either tempera-
ment or literary ideas. Thomas wrote with great facility and followed the literary fashion readily. As a result, he became immensely popular but was quickly forgotten. Pierre, on the other
hand, stuck more to his own ideas, was more personal in his writings, and survived. Yet seldom were two brothers closer in private
life. It is therefore imperative that the reader keep in mind a
certain duality within the life of Pierre Corneille. On the one
hand, there is the good bourgeois, the magistrate, the family man
leading an uneventful life; on the other, a great, proud literary
figure, at times sure of himself and of his destiny, at times groping in the dark for the one path to success and overreacting to
every obstacle, real or imagined.

The literary road traveled by Corneille was one fraught with bifurcations, and it is only a posteriori that the critic can speak of a steady progression. At the very beginning of his career, Corneille hesitated between poetry and the theater. Somewhat later, he had to decide between comedy and tragedy, and even within that last choice there seem to be moments of hesitation, of uncertain reactions to events and changes in public taste. Thus, after many "Cornelian" tragedies, there occurred a softening of lines, a trend broken by the "reactionary" *Nicomède*. As we shall see, Corneille was doubtless moved by a predetermined idea of certain goals, but there were many crises in the author's search for the best method of attaining them. From *Mélite* to *Suréna* it is easy enough to trace a steady curve but not without encountering numerous deviations from the norm, such as *Don Sanche, Andromède*, or *Psyché*.

Corneille's search for a vocation began very early. While still in school, in 1618 and again in 1620 he won prizes for versification in Latin, but he did not give up his law studies. He eventually joined the bar, but his first experience convinced him that he would never make a fortune as a lawyer, and so his parents bought him a post in the magistry. During these early years he wrote numerous poems, occasional and other, and he published some of these in 1632 under the title *Mélanges poétiques*. By that time, however, he had also had a taste of theatrical success, and his career was launched.

The success of *Mélite* (1629) was immediate and catapulted Corneille into the mainstream of literary life. From that time on, the twenty-three-year-old author knew that he was meant for the theater. True, he did at times pen a ballet libretto or an occasional poem, but these excursions were rare, and except for the religious poems of his later years, Corneille became a dramatist. Ironically, this position is made most manifest in two of the aforementioned excursions, "Excuse à Ariste" and "Excusatio," in which he begged to be excused from having to write non-dramatic poetry because he had found his niche writing for the stage.[1] But within the framework of dramaturgy Corneille was still groping, as a quick glance at his early plays will manifest. Of his first eight plays, only five are unequivocally comedies (*Mélite, La Veuve, La Galerie du Palais, La Suivante, La Place Royalle*, to which should be added Corneille's contribution to *La Comédie des Tuileries*); *L'Illusion comique* was called a comedy by the author who, as a matter of fact, dropped the last word from the title later, for it is really a tragicomedy; *Clitandre* was originally called a tragicomedy, then tragedy; *Médée* was called tragedy but, as we shall see later on, does not completely deserve that appellation. It should further be noted that, while five of the eight plays fit into a single classification, that classification is a very large one allowing for a very broad spectrum of tones, characters, and moods. One therefore gets the picture of a young author in search of himself, a search made all the more difficult by public caprice; in the five years between *Mélite* and *Médée* a great number of tragicomedies, a plethora of pastorals, but only a half-dozen tragedies were created in France. Within a decade, that order was inverted, which may have had much to do with Corneille finding his proper niche, and even more with his retitling of plays such as *Clitandre* and *Le Cid*.

Just as these early years show Corneille in search of a vocation, they also show him in quest of a patron. The occasional poetry, the ballet librettos, the dedications of his plays, each one to a different potential protector, all are ample indications of this unsuccessful hunt. In the seventeenth century, a Maecenas not only provided a livelihood to the artist, it also accorded the relationship between the two that was essential to their way of life. The aristocrat owed it to his concept of self to support the finer things in life. In return, the creative artist became the patron's creature in more ways than one. It is this last aspect of the relationship that explains Corneille's problems in finding a proper protector.

Corneille led the peaceful and banal life of a typical Norman bourgeois even after the king conferred a title on the family. But —and this too is typical of the class whence he came—Corneille was extremely jealous of his freedom and proud of his capabilities. For such a man subservience, real or feigned, would have been very difficult to accept and artistic dictatorship unacceptable. Therefore, Corneille frequented many of the fashionable literary salons of the day but became attached to none. Only one patron —Richelieu—managed to force a yoke of some kind on Corneille, but even that relationship did not last long.[2]

If any attachment can be seen in the early days of Corneille's dramatic career, it is the one he formed with the dramatic group eventually known as the theater of the Marais. To better understand this relationship it is necessary to comprehend the situation of the theatrical world in Paris at the beginning of the century. For some time the *Confrérie de la Passion,* a group of worthy bourgeois, had had the monopoly of serious secular drama in Paris and the suburbs, by virtue of a royal privilege. The brotherhood no longer performed but instead leased their locale—later to be known as the Hôtel de Bourgogne—to actors who thus enjoyed the right to be the sole permanent troupe in the capital. Other troupes could, and did, lease various tennis courts, and were allowed to perform as long as they paid the *Confrérie,* but such contracts were temporary. As a result, many professional troupes of actors joined the innumerable amateurs in making provincial theatrical life as active as that of the capital. Many of these troupes included Paris in their itinerary, of course, and one of these, in 1625, came to stay, fighting the established "royal comedians" for the exclusive right to use the Hôtel de Bourgogne. By 1629, however, it too had disappeared.

In the summer of 1629, a seasoned troupe of actors led by the already famous Montdory passed through Rouen. Young Corneille showed the manuscript of his first play, *Mélite,* to Montdory who accepted it and took it to Paris where his troupe scored an impressive triumph with it. It was the beginning of a relationship unique in seventeenth-century annals: as André Stegmann has stated,[3] the history of Corneille's dramatic career until the mid-1640's is also the history of this troupe, eventually called "of the Marais" because it settled in that section of Paris in 1634. So close was the relationship that it influenced the composition of Corneille's plays: there can be no doubt that the unusual distribution of roles—great number of women for instance—is a direct reflection of the make-up of the Marais company.[4]

II *The Five Authors*

As has already been noted, Corneille tried his hand at almost every type of drama, often defying public taste by his very choice, but with remarkable success. As a result, he was asked by Richelieu to join L'Estoile, Rotrou, Boisrobert, and Colletet—all men of reputation and merit—in forming the famous company of the "Five Authors." Richelieu, who had literary aspirations of his own, suggested the topics and the five authors wrote the plays. Their first joint effort, the *Comédie des Tuileries* (1635), was written in a single month, was magnificently staged, had a limited success, but was not published until three years later. In all likelihood Corneille contributed Act III. In January 1637, he again collaborated on such a joint venture, the *Grande pastorale,* which was such a failure that it was suppressed by mutual consent. The following month Corneille contributed the first act to the *Aveugle de Smyrne.* In 1638 he began but never finished his share of *Mirame,* and by 1641, when it was performed, Desmarests was listed as the sole author "protected" by Richelieu.

Much ink has been spilled over Corneille's bolting the "Five," and the entire truth will probably never be known. Was it pride and an independent spirit? Was it Richelieu's role in the quarrel of the *Cid?* Undoubtedly Corneille's joining—and eventually leaving—the "Five" is but one facet of a very complex relationship which is all too often boiled down to the central episode that is the quarrel of the *Cid.* While it is true that Corneille had refused to contribute to an anthology of poems dedicated to Richelieu, there must have been a grudging mutual esteem, witness Corneille's subsequent joining of the "Five." Furthermore, it was not Richelieu who started the famous quarrel but Corneille's rivals, Scudéry and Mairet, equally incensed by the success of *Cid* and its author's vainglorious attitude. Scudéry's *Observations sur le Cid* (1637) threatened to really envenom the dispute when Richelieu intervened by asking the newly created French Academy to critique the play. He had seen the play several times (twice during command performances), and it is therefore likely that he saw in the burgeoning affair not so much a chance to crush the young upstart as one to allow the even younger Academy to prove its mettle and establish its authority. This is why Richelieu rejected the first draft of the critique for its lack of firmness. Long before the printing of the final draft, the debate had reached such scandalous levels that Richelieu was forced to impose silence on all concerned. The appearance of the *Sentiments* (1638) satisfied no one: the pedantic document quibbled over petty rules and insignificant details, showing the savants' unwillingness or inability to see the genius made manifest to all of France. As Guez de Balzac put it, it is one thing to produce a work entirely within the rules; it is quite another to produce one that wins the suffrage of an entire country. The public had declared Corneille an easy winner; the Academy fundamentally avoided the verdict.

The aftermath of the quarrel is no less ambiguous. On the one hand, Richelieu allowed the printing of the *Sentiments* while imposing silence on all individuals including Corneille, who must have wanted to reply. He also, after the dissolution of the "Five," gave his full support to Desmarests, one of Corneille's most ardent foes. On the other hand Richelieu granted Corneille a pension of 1500 *livres*. In January 1637, Corneille's father was granted letters of nobility, a favor that would not have been possible had these two great men really been at odds. Furthermore, *Horace,* Corneille's first play after the *Cid*, was premiered at a private performance at the home of Richelieu, who also accepted the dedication of the play. The most logical conclusion, then, would be that Corneille, proud and sure of his talents, refused to bow to the wishes of the cardinal and become a hack in a stable of literary mediocrities. Richelieu, equally proud, undoubtedly tried to lower Corneille's stock and, to some extent, succeeded. Corneille must have sensed these motives and respected his adversary, for at the death of Richelieu he penned a bittersweet poem which neither lauded nor blamed. A quatrain attributed to him states the same feelings even more succinctly:

> Qu'on parle mal ou bien du fameux Cardinal,
> Ma prose ni mes vers n'en diront jamais rien:
> Il m'a fait trop de bien pour en dire du mal,
> Il m'a fait trop de mal pour en dire du bien. (X, 86)

(Whether people speak well or ill of the famous Cardinal,
Neither my prose nor my verse will ever say anything about him:
He did me too much good to speak ill of him,
He did me too much harm to say anything good.)

III *The Years of the Tetrology*

Corneille's otherwise steady production was punctuated by several "silences," periods during which he produced no new plays. The first such break occurred in 1637 after the quarrel of the *Cid*. Much has been made of it; perhaps too much. To be sure, three years lapsed before the appearance of *Horace*, but they were far from empty. The quarrel and the two efforts on behalf of the "Five" must have taken up much of Corneille's time in 1637. The following year, his job made some unusual demands on the consc-i entious man, and it had to be defended against a rival, a second lawyer named to the "marble table." Early in 1639 Corneille's father died, and in July of that year the bloody "nu-pieds" rebellion started in Normandy. In spite of all that, by November 1639, Corneille read *Horace* to a group of friends. Furthermore, the fact that *Horace, Cinna,* and *Polyeucte* appeared in quick succession suggests that the silence imposed on Corneille by circumstances had been far from sterile. Although Chapelain, during the quarrel of the *Cid,* bemoaned the fact that Scudéry might have silenced Corneille, it is far more probable that this silence was due to the aforementioned circumstances and perhaps also to Corneille's groping for a new avenue which, once found, led to a veritable flood of new plays.

The history of *Polyeucte* shows that, at that time, its author was still quite unsure of that avenue: the play was first read in public at the Hôtel de Rambouillet, then one of the most brilliant of literary gatherings; when it failed to win the approval of those present, Corneille tried to withdraw the play which was already in rehearsal, and only the actors' pleas dissuaded him. Much of the criticism was, in fact, ill-founded. For instance, some of the contemporaries blamed him for putting Christianity on stage. In this they merely showed their ignorance of theatrical history, for religion had been a major ingredient of both medieval and Renaissance drama, and Corneille was merely continuing a tradition of long standing. Nor was he alone in this, and the list of plays written in the first half of the seventeenth century includes many religious plays by a wide variety of authors.

IV   *Troubled Years*

The years following the production of *Horace, Cinna,* and *Polyeucte* were very eventful for Corneille. In 1641 he married Marie de Lampérière. In 1642 Richelieu died, and Louis XIII revoked all literary pensions, temporarily placing Corneille in an uncomfortable though far from impoverished position. One year later Mazarin, Richelieu's heir, renewed Corneille's pension, but, unlike his predecessor, the new minister had no literary ambitions and therefore refrained from creating an authors' clique. Corneille might have given even more of himself to the Marais as a result, but here too, events were to dictate otherwise. During the 1640–41 and 1641–42 seasons, that troupe had produced *Horace, Cinna,* and *Polyeucte.* It disbanded at Easter, 1642. When it regrouped some time later it had lost some of its best members, starting a decline that was to have an indisputable influence on Corneille's production. Thus *Rodogune,* reflecting the changes in available actors, has only four male parts, two of which are minor ones. In 1645, as though consecrating the decline of the Marais, Corneille allowed the Bourgogne players to produce *Rodogune.* In the meantime, Corneille had written *Le Menteur* and *La Suite du Menteur,* but, be it inclination or the demise of the Marais troupe, there were to be no more true comedies. This does not mean that Corneille abandoned the Marais completely, for in 1647 *Héraclius* was premiered by that troupe. However, later that year Floridor, one of the stars of the Marais, assumed the directorship of the Bourgogne players, and *Héraclius* seemingly moved with him. That Corneille's inner travails were far from over is made apparent by the chronology of his production. After *Héraclius* (January, 1647) there was a rather long silence, then *Don Sanche* (1649), a "heroic comedy," followed by *Andromède,* a fantastic *pièce à machines,* both obvious concessions to public taste. Then came *Nicomède,* the "synthesis of a Cornelian decade,"[5] followed by *Pertharite,* an anachronism at best. Then there was a relapse into silence.

To be sure, this silence had many reasons, as we shall see, and not all of them were literary. In 1644 and again in 1646, Corneille's candidacy to the French Academy had been rejected possibly because he did not reside in the capital, one of the requirements of membership. In 1647, date of Floridor's change of allegiance and of *Héraclius,* Corneille promised to move to Paris. Séguier, one of the most powerful men in France and protector of the Academy, saw to it that "his" candidate Ballesdens withdrew, and Corneille was elected as *Héraclius* triumphed at the Bourgogne. When the play was published that year it was dedicated to Séguier with the usual laudatory remarks and some political pronouncements which showed Corneille's royalist tendencies and his admiration for those working for the greater glory of France. This is particularly interesting because the Fronde was about to begin. When, within six months of the death of Richelieu, Louis XIII died, leaving the throne to the infant Louis XIV, both the great nobles and the Parlement of Paris felt that changes were imminent. It must be kept in mind that the Parlement of Paris had only its name in common with its English counterpart: its job was not to make laws but to register and administer them. Even in this limited capacity it had been constantly thwarted by Richelieu and Louis XIII, who had repeatedly seen to it that the Parlement could not interfere with the running of "their" state. Shortly before his death Louis XIII had made a will providing for a regency council which included, in addition to the queen-mother, Mazarin and Gaston d'Orléans—the former a wily Italian, the latter the very unreliable brother of the king—as well as princes of the blood and members of the king's government. When Anne of Austria, the queen-mother, asked the Parlement to set aside that will and declare her sole regent (an act for which there was ample historical precedent), Mazarin assured its members that this would guarantee future cooperation between the regent and Parlement. As a result, Parlement felt itself confirmed in its political stand and was only too happy to set aside the king's will. However, as the saying of the time went, the queen hated work and loved Mazarin, and so the latter soon had all the power that had once been Richelieu's and perhaps even more. In fact, Mazarin became the actual ruler of France.

This rule was far from satisfactory, and within five years both the princes of the blood and the upper middle class were weary of it. War and graft had taken their toll of the economy, and in 1648 Parlement decided to make itself the voice of the general discontent. The basic question raised once again was whether the king's power was the result of some sort of social contract or whether it emanated from "the grace of God." On the surface, the demands made by the Parlement in June, 1648, seem purely administrative; in fact, they would have meant the rule of law as opposed to that of the "good pleasure" of the king, or of Mazarin. The regent hesitated, then had the leaders of Parlement arrested. At once barricades went up in Paris. The queen feigned to yield, but as soon as possible she took the young king and fled. The Parlement was ill-equipped for a revolutionary struggle, and soon the fight against Mazarin and the queen became the plaything of aristocratic soldiers. In the comic-opera struggle that followed, guiding principles gave way to personal capriciousness and anarchy. People, moved by ambition or pride, changed sides as one might change shirts. By comparison, Mazarin appeared as a paragon of patriotism and loyalty.

This devastating game—anything but funny to the common people—lasted five years. By 1653, France lay in ruins. By feigning to yield, Mazarin, who had twice gone into exile but without ever relinquishing his hold on the regent, weathered the storm. It has been said that he literally wore out the opposition. Whether one admires or despises Mazarin, it must be acknowledged that by his actions he reduced the aristocracy to a servile state from which it was never to recover. The Parlement, having fumbled its chances, was discredited. When, at the death of Mazarin, Louis XIV said that he was the state, he was merely consecrating a situation that had been realized in 1653.

Throughout this period Corneille never wavered in his support of the monarchy, the queen-mother, and Mazarin. During the early years, he was at home in Rouen, working on several plays simultaneously. In 1649 *Don Sanche* failed miserably, possibly because of its theme which pitted a virtuous man of relatively low origins against aristocrats of far lesser merit. Some critics have suggested that the play failed because Mazarin, considering it too revolutionary and suggestive in those troubled times, wished it to, but Mazarin's credit could not have been very great in 1649. In January, 1650, *Andromède,* a grandiose *pièce à machines,* was produced during a short respite in the revolution. A spectacular, though mediocre, play, its success was undoubtedly due to the contemporary taste for the fastuous. Later that year or very early in 1651, Corneille wrote what is perhaps his purest drama *Nicomède*. Love, fear, horror—none of the Aristotelian commonplaces are present. The *intérêt* of the play is centered exclusively on admiration, and the play has been rightfully considered Corneille's absolute statement on the triumph of will. The noble hero of the play, surrounded by a world of mediocrities—is this the monarchy prey to the baying *Frondeurs?* The parallel is certainly tempting. What Robert Brasillach has called a conglomeration of fear, of rampant envy, of underhanded crime, of dirt and imbecility [6]—is this not the very essence of self-seeking adventurers such as La Grande Mademoiselle and Gondi? [7] In *Nicomède,* Arsinoë and Prusias opposing Nicomède can easily be seen as the underhanded, self-seeking, undecided mediocrities of the Frondeur party opposed by the unwavering purpose and self-assertion of the Royalists. Nicomède, as Robert Brasillach has so well shown, is a brash youngster showing his elders what honor and rectitude are all about; he is the very incarnation of grandeur and of majesty, and the play that bears his name clearly reveals that, while Corneille might have liked Mazarin and his cause, he had not forgotten Richelieu and his methods. However, it would be wrong to conclude that Corneille had second thoughts concerning Richelieu. He had always been a staunch Royalist—"The worst of states is a popular state" (*Cinna*, 521)—and the full meaning of that word as applied to him can be seen in the part he played in the composition of *Les Triomphes de Louis le Juste*. As of 1645, a letter signed by the young King had asked Corneille to contribute to a volume in honor of Louis XIII. The work appeared in 1649, in mid-Fronde, and Corneille's contributions— twenty epigrams explaining Valdor's engravings—describe the reign of Louis XIII as though it had been a purely personal one: there is one flattering mention of Mazarin, none of Richelieu!

Faithful servant of the crown, Corneille was rewarded with a lucrative post. But in the meanwhile he had given up his other charges; thus, when in 1651 he was obliged to surrender his new post, he was left without any magisterial ties. Shortly thereafter he saw the dismal failure of *Pertharite*, his last play until *Œdipe*, in 1659. This period of "silence," like the one that began in 1637, has been thoroughly studied by every Cornelian scholar, and again it must be said that many of these have overstated its importance or overdramatized its possible causes.

Robert Brasillach has suggested that Corneille's diary for the seven years of this "retreat" is the *Imitation de Jésus-Christ*.[8] This opinion—not original to Brasillach and often repeated after that— fails to take into account even the simplest matters of chronological truth. As of 1651 Corneille had published the first twenty chapters of this religious poem whose first complete edition came out in 1656. He did not retire to write it, nor did he come out of retirement after its completion; the cause, or causes, of the retirement is one thing; its effects were another. In his foreword to *Pertharite*, Corneille announced not only his retreat but its reason: "The bad reception given this work warns me that it is time for me to sound the retreat." Quoting Horace, he felt that by insisting he would only manage to make himself ridiculous. He was, nevertheless, justifiably proud of what he had done for the theater. In this letter, written early in 1653, there is no pique but rather the feeling that perhaps the times had passed him by.[9] And so Corneille stopped writing plays for a while, but he did not abandon the theater for all that, or mundane matters as a whole. During these years Corneille's friend, Pellisson, was writing a history of the French Academy. When he stated that Corneille had agreed to the Academy's arbitration of the *Cid* question, Corneille raised vehement objections, showing that he kept in touch with such matters. At the same time, he worked repeatedly on his past plays, making numerous corrections for the editions of his complete works that kept on appearing at regular intervals. He also began to write the three "discours"—one for each of three volumes —and the *Examens*—one for each play—for the 1660 edition. In these he expounded his critical theories, the result of many years of writing for and thinking about the stage.[10] In addition to these theatrical endeavors, Corneille wrote numerous liminary poems for his friends' books, and occasional poems dating from that period are plentiful. Furthermore, the fact that *Œdipe* did not appear until 1659 should not be overstressed. As of July, 1656, he had accepted a commission to write the spectacular *Toison d'or*. The delay is easy to explain: Corneille had been ill for some time —in 1654 he had even gone to take the waters at Bourbon—and so had his wife. In 1657 his brother Antoine died, and his mother died the following year. Yet, by the end of that year, *Œdipe* was finished.

Despite this profane activity, the major work of Corneille for these years remains the *Imitation*. One look at the over thirteen thousand lines will convince anyone of the magnitude of the task to which Corneille had set himself. Magnitude, however, should not be mistaken for intensity. The *Imitation* is a conscientious job of translation and versification by a conscientious churchwarden. But it would be a very thankless task to seek in it any sign of personal involvement, of intense lyricism, or, as Robert Brasillach would have us believe, of an active quest for God. True, the work contains many condemnations of the mundane pleasures praised in Corneille's theater, but is that "naïve duplicity" [11] or just the careful craftsman and translator rendering unto Caesar that which is his? Is it "puerile candor" [12] or the epitome of artifice? While it will not settle the argument, it is interesting to remember that exercises such as this were extremely popular and lucrative. The success of the partial editions—the first twenty chapters in 1651, eleven more in 1652, the first two books in 1653, the first thirty chapters of book three in 1654—must have consoled Corneille and helped him forget his last dramatic failure, and when the complete *Imitation* had four separate editions in 1656 alone, Corneille must have felt more than the gratitude of a devout believer.[13]

V *In Search of Renewal*

In 1659, with *Œdipe*, Corneille not only reëntered the theatrical lists, but he did so with a new vigor and combative spirit. In 1658 Fouquet, the wealthy financial secretary, had given Corneille three topics from which to choose. Giving two of these to his brother, Corneille took the third, that of Oedipus, and in a few months wrote what was to be one of his greater successes. The success, however, was short-lived. The play was, if not a compromise, at least an attempt to follow the tastes of the day, to refer to the topics of discussion then in vogue. Fouquet, an anti-Jansenist, must have been pleased with Corneille's treatment of the question of free choice and responsibility. The primacy of love in the play must have pleased not only all the aging *précieux*, but also those who, just a few years later, would welcome with open arms Racine's *Alexandre*. It goes without saying that these are the very factors which make the modern reader relegate the play to a not totally undeserved limbo.

Late the following year, Corneille had another ephemeral success with *La Toison d'or*, one of his most spectacular *pièces à machines* which the Marais troupe took to Paris in 1661. Perhaps as a result of this success the Marais also premiered Corneille's next play, *Sertorius*, in 1662. Interestingly enough, the play was a critical success but not a popular one. To fully understand this it is necessary to go back to 1659 and Corneille's return to the stage.

One critic has suggested that from *Œdipe* on, Corneille dared with each new play to investigate new dramatic avenues as if to see how far he could go and still keep the crowds faithful.[14] Only one reservation must be made: while some plays show bold innovations, others appear as strangely anachronistic, and therein lies the tale. The key year, if a single date is to be designated, is 1661. In that fateful year Mazarin died and Fouquet was arrested. With the death of Mazarin, the "age of Louis XIII" that Corneille understood so well came to an end. With the fall of Fouquet Corneille lost what little contact he had with the new reign. Yet his plays had had a tremendous success, and so it should not surprise us that he decided to forego the idea of a Maecenas and strike out boldly on his own, hoping to ride the wave of success. Thus, in 1662 he left a cousin in charge of his Rouen affairs and with his brother Thomas returned to settle in Paris. Shortly before, he had written *Sertorius,* which he undoubtedly considered the acid test of public opinion. As I have already stated, the public did not agree with the critics' praise. Both foes and friends alike were probably thrown off balance by the absence of what Corneille, in the prefatory letter, called "tenderness of love, passionate out-bursts, pompous descriptions, pathetic narrations." They were do-ing what so many critics have done since: judging the late plays not on their intrinsic merits but on how well they remained faithful to the esthetics established in the earlier ones. The success of *So-phonisbe* in 1663 was equally mixed, perhaps because the char-acters of the play are all too often impure, never quite sure of their roles as heroic lovers or loving heroes. Corneille's answer to this public reaction was *Othon,* a lucid, bitter, chilling play of political machinations in which love has no place at all. The out-come of this clever game of rival intelligences is of little or no concern to the reader or viewer who, without fear or pity, is com-pelled merely by the admiration he may have for the brilliantly Machiavellian protagonists created by a man who had always been hostile to Machiavellianism. If we are to believe Corneille, a few solid minds gave their suffrage to *Othon,* but the play failed to gain popular support.

This inability to obtain popular success was not the only bitter pill Corneille had to swallow in these crucial years. In 1663 two senior members of the Academy, Costar and Chapelain, had been charged to draw up lists of those writers of the realm most worthy of receiving pensions. Although Costar was most lauda-tory—he obtained for Corneille a pension of two thousand *livres* for being the "world's greatest dramatic poet"—Chapelain was less so. Corneille never forgave Chapelain for this reticence, and in his thanks to the king, he took delight in paraphrasing Chapelain's less than enthusiastic remarks in great lines of mock humility. In the closing paragraph of this *"Remerciment au Roi"* he offered his further services to the king, asking to be performed at court so that he might "regain his exhausted vigor," but the king liked comedy too much and chose to honor Molière instead.

One year later, in 1664, a royal edict canceled all acts of nobility granted since 1634. It will be remembered that Corneille's elevation had been in 1637. Corneille protested both in verse and in person, and in 1665 Louis XIV reconfirmed the gift originally made by his father. Corneille celebrated the new honors by buying a captaincy for his oldest son and a lieutenancy for the younger. He then wrote a marvelously pompous praise for the return of the victorious king from Flanders. In this poem he again reminded the reader of his past glories, wishing for new ones:

> Que ne peuvent, grand Roi, tes hautes destinées
> Me rendre la vigueur de mes jeunes années!
> Qu'ainsi qu'au temps du *Cid* je ferois de jaloux!   (X, 187)

> (Why can't, o great King, your great deeds
> Give me back the strength of my youth!
> How many, as in the days of the *Cid*, I would make jealous!)

Never had Corneille written more prophetic lines: the rest of his life was one long struggle against creeping obscurity. Like so many of his heroes, he was desperately trying to re-create himself, to dazzle Versailles and Paris with innovative ideas, but his success was never again to be more than partial.

Othon had been but a partial success. *Agésilas*, in 1666, was a dismal failure. It may be that Corneille, having just lost his son Charles, had not put his whole heart in the composition of the play, which is very prosaic. It may also be that the public was not ready for a play in free verse which, despite its subtitle, was more heroic comedy than tragedy. Even his staunchest admirers, such as Saint-Evremond, considered him passé and looked to the young Racine—whose *Alexandre le Grand* had just scored a resounding success—to carry the standard of French tragedy. When, in 1667, *Attila* triumphed, circumstances again prevented Corneille from enjoying the victory, for the year of *Attila* was also the year of the Du Parc defection.

From the beginning, Molière had performed Corneille's plays, often reviving many of the better early ones. Thus, in 1662, his troupe performed, among others, *Héraclius*, *Rodogune*, and *Sertorius*, the first two being plays that Corneille considered highly though they had not been too successful. Molière premiered several of Corneille's plays, and the two authors collaborated on *Psyché*. One other tie existed between the two playwrights: Corneille was in love with the star of Molière's troupe, Mlle Du Parc. He was not alone in this, for Molière had been his predecessor and Racine was to supplant them both. At any rate, Molière and Racine having quarreled, the latter withdrew his hit *Alexandre,* giving it to the actors of the Hôtel de Bourgogne. Soon after, Mlle Du Parc, who had created the role of Axiane in the play, passed to the rival troupe, no doubt succumbing to the pleas of Racine himself. And so, precisely at the moment when Corneille could have used her talents to shore up his slipping prestige, she passed to the enemy. Corneille, as he had done before, retreated into a silence broken only by the publication of *L'Office de la Sainte Vierge,* a very uneven mixture of pious prose and platitudinous verse, and ended late in 1670 with the appearance of *Tite et Bérénice.* In the meanwhile Mlle Du Parc, the woman who had played such an important role—on the personal as well as the professional level—in the rivalry between the two greatest writers of tragedies, had died in 1668. Both men were heartbroken, but the rivalry survived.

The bitterness of this rivalry has at times been overstated. Corneille and Racine represent not only two different points of view but two different generations. Corneille's stiffening resistance to the "new wave" was not a blind one, and he fully recognized that many of his recent endeavors had been "against the taste of the times." [15] Furthermore, he tried at least once, in *Tite et Bérénice,* to be "Racinian," and although he failed, it reveals a certain regard for his rival. Corneille's fairness toward his rival is further attested to by the fact that he joined his colleagues in unanimously electing Racine to the Academy in 1672. By the same token, Racine generally behaved properly toward his older rival. Only once, in the preface to *Britannicus,* did he go beyond the bounds of propriety, but even there friends prevailed on him to suppress the vitriolic diatribe, and the second preface, though by no means friendly, was greatly toned down. To be sure, the rivalry was intense, and if Corneille tried to best Racine at his own game, the latter reciprocated with *Mithridate,* certainly not his most successful play. In their haste to best each other both playwrights treated the same theme—*Tite et Bérénice* by Corneille, *Bérénice* by Racine—each one rushing his play to publication, though there the similarity ends: with thirty consecutive performances, Racine's play was a smash hit, whereas after eight per-

formances of *Tite et Bérénice* Molière had to show his own
Bourgeois gentilhomme on alternate nights. Racine, like his rival,
knew how to be fair. Thus, when *Iphigénie* was first produced at
Versailles in 1674, Racine waited to bring it to Paris until *Suréna,*
Corneille's swan song, had been premiered there, and as Corneille had been able to fight for Racine's membership in the
Academy so was Racine able to sincerely eulogize Corneille upon
his death. Racine was a shrewd polemicist, and he must have
sensed that Corneille was not his worst enemy. Far more dangerous to the ambitious Racine must have been the legion of petty
snipers such as Pradon or Donneau de Visé, who were only too
anxious to malign and assail either Corneille or Racine. Still more
dangerous than Corneille was his brother Thomas, whose star
was rising at that time.

Thomas could be considered as an interesting barometer of the
fortunes of the Corneille-Racine dilemma. Until 1672 he had written plays that could be labeled Cornelian; but that year he published *Ariane,* the first of his Racinian works. That is also the year
of *Pulchérie* by his brother Pierre. Read first at the home of the
Duc de La Rochefoucauld, then at that of the Cardinal de Retz—
both members of the "old school" and witnesses of his earlier
triumphs—*Pulchérie,* a heroic comedy, shows that Pierre, unlike
Thomas, had decided to continue the fight against the general
trends. Be it because of a lackluster performance by the mori-
bund Marais, or because of the anachronistic subject—the politically motivated marriage of a princess, a topic admittedly against
"the taste of the times"—the play was a dismal failure. Not only
had the public been won over to Racine, but the king too, though
Colbert, his minister, who never forgave Corneille for his attachment to Fouquet, might have had something to do with that. It
must be further admitted that tragedy as a genre had lost much
of its popularity, and here again Thomas' production is a valid
measuring stick: after 1672, though he does not abandon pure
tragedy, he indulges more and more in the writing of operas,
comedies, and *pièces à machines,* the popular genres. Racine
persisted until 1677, the year of *Phèdre.* As for Pierre Corneille,
his last effort was *Suréna* in 1674, the year—ironically—in which
the king revoked his pension.

The very content of *Suréna* bespeaks of weariness. It too, like
the preceding plays, was an anachronism: Corneille, all the while

seeing the changes in public taste, had continued his own evolutionary pattern adding to each hero what wisdom he had acquired himself. Suréna, like Rodrigue, sees the need of the hero to constantly face new challenges, but Suréna is a much older man, weary of a life in which one must always "love, suffer, die" (348). Seldom had Corneille written a more biographical line. His twenty-two-year-old son had just met a heroic death at Grave; his pension (to be restored in 1682) was revoked; the public no longer rushed to his plays. Yet like his last hero,[16] Corneille had a just concept of his merit. When in 1676 the king had *Cinna, Horace, Pompée, Œdipe, Sertorius,* and *Rodogune* performed at Versailles, Corneille wrote a poem to thank him. Scarcely believing that his former triumphs were not being dimmed by the light shed by his younger rivals, he suggested that the king now turn to the later works, and surely there is more than the demand of rhyme that made him link *Cinna* and *Suréna*. Speaking of his age, of his last plays as "the last spark of a fire about to die out," [17] he admits that his fire still wishes to dazzle, to "*éblouir.*" That is the key word. Speaking of the works of Corneille, the eminent critic Jean Starobinski has said that in them everything begins with "*éblouissement.*" [18] This statement is no less true for Corneille himself. Like his heroes, he continuously tried to re-create himself, to renew his glory, to shine, to appear as great as he knew himself to be. Unfortunately, neither the king nor the general public were listening or watching. Although his plays were still performed with some frequency, the *Gazette* of April 27, 1680, in announcing a new benefice for Corneille, felt obliged to identify the recipient as a man "who forty years ago wrote some tragedies that are still performed before the King." By then, it must be admitted that Corneille had retired from the fray, retouching his works—too much at times, as we shall see in Chapter 2—and slowly sinking into what even his kind nephew Fontenelle had to call senility. The ultimate irony is that during the last days of his life Corneille could not be aware of a revival in popularity of his plays. He died during the night of September 30, 1684. Less than two months later his brother Thomas took his place at the Academy, welcomed by Racine who took the opportunity to praise the departed with words that still ring true today: "You know in what condition was the French stage when he began his work. Such disorder! such irregularity! No taste, no knowledge of the real

beauties of the theater . . . In this chaos, [. . . Corneille]
against the bad taste of the century, . . . inspired by an extraordinary genius, . . . put reason on stage, but a reason acompanied by
all the pomp and all the ornaments of which our language is
capable; happily uniting verisimilitude and the marvelous, he
left far behind him all the rivals . . . who tried in vain, through
their discourses and frivolous criticism, to lower a merit that they
could not equal." [19]

CHAPTER 2

The Comic Illusion

"SUCH disorder, such irregularity!" Racine may or may not have thought of the very first plays of Corneille, but there is no doubt that comedy in the late 1620's was of the lowest order, and Corneille was quite right in boasting, as he did in the *Examen* of *Mélite* which he penned decades later, that this play was really the first to be written for *honnestes gens* (gentlemen and ladies) and that, if it at times seemed to violate rules and unities, that was because they had not yet been established.

These early plays are a strange mixture of influences and independence. The influence of Hardy, one of Corneille's most prolific contemporaries, is readily seen in the violent melodrama of *Clitandre,* or in the numerous amorous deceptions scattered throughout all the early comedies. The effects of Italian comedy and of the pastoral vogue on Corneille cannot be denied either; witness the very names of the protagonists—Tirsis, Cloris, Lisis, Mélite, and so on. These influences, however, tend to be rather superficial, and even though Corneille did little to revolutionize the world of drama in the early 1630's, he did much to further the most salutary trends. To be sure, Corneille is a child of his times, and the ostentation, the illusion, the metamorphoses, the instability, all the commonplaces of Baroque literature are omnipresent in these early works. This is not only true of the content of the plays but of their form as well. It can truly be said that from *Mélite* to *Le Cid,* a period of some seven years during which he produced ten plays, Corneille was in constant search of a form. The fact that *Le Cid* was first called "tragicomedy" (an error that Corneille quickly corrected) is further indication of that. Call it Baroque or Romanesque, until *Le Cid* there is a certain exaltation, a youthful brio in these early plays which Corneille will never again be able to capture, not even in the verbal exuberance of later comedies such as *Le Menteur.* Thus, Corneille in search of

Corneille is many things, unafraid as he is to borrow from everyone and everything that surrounds him. But he is above all, even
in these early days, a man of taste. The psychological realism of
Clitandre more than overshadows the borrowings from Hardy's
shallow melodramas. Whereas Hardy had relied heavily on visual
effects, Corneille used them but sparingly. The names of the first
protagonists may recall those of the pastoral, but *Mélite,* as well
as the later plays, is populated by gentle people who do not feel
the need to disguise themselves in the ubiquitous shepherd's
clothes, and for that alone Corneille deserves our gratitude. By
the same token all the banal and gratuitous tricks of the theatrical
trade are present in the plays—false letters; scenes of madness,
real or feigned; commonplaces of words, plot, and character—but
they are invariably enhanced by a grace and elegance of language
and a psychological insight previously unknown in France.

I *Mélite*

Racine, when it came to plots, prided himself on "making
something of nothing"; the same cannot be said of Corneille, as
can be seen by the synopsis of *Mélite,* his first play. Eraste intro-
duces Mélite, whom he loves, to his friend Tirsis, only to become
jealous. To remedy the situation he sends some love letters (supposedly from Mélite) to Philandre, who is betrothed to Cloris, the
sister of Tirsis. Philandre, thanks to the artifice and the persuasive
powers of Eraste, decides to leave Cloris for Mélite and shows the
letters of Tirsis. In despair the latter withdraws to the home of a
friend, Lisis, who spreads false rumors of Tirsis' death. Mélite
faints at the news. Thus assured of Mélite's true feelings, Lisis
reunites the two lovers. However Cliton, having seen Mélite in a
faint, believes her dead too, and spreads the news of this "double
death" to Eraste, who goes mad with remorse. Brought back to his
senses by the Nourrice, he asks forgiveness and obtains from the
two lovers not only his pardon but the hand of Cloris, who has
rejected Philandre because of his fickleness.

The complexities of the plot are at times aggravated by a language that has often been characterized as overly distilled and
ostentatious. While there is much truth in that, it must be kept in
mind that the language is not Corneille's but that of the fashionable dandy of the era and thus contributes no little to the verisimilitude of the characters. In this respect, it is rather unfortunate

that in later years Corneille, responding to criticism prompted either by jealousy or by changing taste, toned down the language of his earlier days, and in so doing eradicated the very essence of the gallant world of the 1620's and 1630's that he had so beautifully depicted. While the secondary characters are seldom imbued with any relief and seem rather flat, the four main ones sparkle. Of particular interest is Tirsis. The world of *Mélite* is a highly mercurial one in which few things are certain and in which a protagonist might be readily forgiven for not wanting to involve himself with his fellow creatures. But while a Philandre wallows in a cowardly and self-indulging narcissism, Tirsis is saved by his love. Upon the backdrop of constant interplay between truth and sham, between appearance and reality—in words and deeds—Tirsis moves not toward deception and eventually self-deception, but away from it. In the first scene Tirsis appears as a man who seeks only tangible gains, who deceives so as not to be deceived, and who is sure that all a woman's beauty will not turn him against the notion that constancy is a folly (135–36). But this gay young blade's notions are soon reduced to nothing when he is dazzled by Mélite. What exactly has he seen? "I saw I know not what" (354). Mélite has but to appear for Tirsis to realize that it is the tangible gain that is an illusion. The new evidence, the new truth is in her beauty. This is not a metamorphosis of sham into verity or being opposed to appearance; rather, it is being expressed in appearance.[1] Tirsis, at the beginning, opposed beauty to his "truth." He now sees that truth and beauty are but one and the same thing, that "to see Mélite is to love her." [2] Henceforth for Tirsis, as for Mélite, there can be no deception. The dazzlement is not the result of trickery nor does it lead to it;—it leads to a new, deeper vision of reality which brings about the inevitable defeat of trickery and deception.

II *Clitandre*

Corneille had no sooner found success with the formula of *Mélite* than he sought to shine in an entirely different vein. *Clitandre* is a tragicomedy, the most popular dramatic genre at the time. Why did Corneille, so successful with a true comedy, write something so foreign to that initial accomplishment? Most likely it was, as Antoine Adam suggests,[3] not because he courted facile success but because he wanted to leave no challenge unanswered, because he wanted to be the successful rival of the stars of the day. In short, the same notion that made him write a "Racinian" play later on in his life now made him try a tragicomedy replete with all the Romanesque traits then in fashion.

Insofar as plot is concerned, *Mélite* is rather complex. Yet Corneille had synopsized it in less than twenty lines. For *Clitandre,* he wrote an "argument" of over three hundred lines, poking gentle fun at the critics of *Mélite's* plot by exaggerating the complexities of this one. Reduced to its minimum, the story of *Clitandre* is as follows: Caliste and Dorise both love Rosidor who disdains the latter and loves the former. Dorise tries to kill her rival, fails, and is in turn attacked by a jilted lover, Pymante, who had also ambushed Rosidor. A rejected lover of Caliste, Clitandre, is blamed for the ambush, but he is finally recognized as innocent. He winds up in a joyless union with Dorise while Rosidor and Caliste live happily ever after. In the play the plot is anything but simple, and Corneille readily admitted in the preface that the least lapse in attention would result in the viewer, or reader, losing complete track of things.

Such a plot, of course, is typical of most of the tragicomedies of the era. Equally typical is the explicit brutality both in speech and deed: mad transports of anger, attempted murder and rape, an eye put out, and, to cap it off, nature as a whole matching the human violence with a storm of its own. In short, *Clitandre* is full of the type of physical and dithyrambic outbursts that the public was about to reject. For some time yet, this public was to keep its love of declamation, and many plays owed their success as much to great lyrical passages as to dramatic qualities—Tristan L'Hermite's *Mariane* is an excellent example of that—but the monologues of *Clitandre* are extremely passionate, verging on the brutal,[4] and the play was far from successful. Its premiere passed unrecorded, and it had only three separate editions, the first in 1632, the last in 1689. As of 1644 it was included by Corneille in his collected works, but much reworked.[5] In its revised version the play is somewhat toned down, but it remains a strange mixture of unexpected bedfellows, the most incongruous juxtaposition deriving from two tendencies that Corneille was to maintain in his work for a long time and which are, to some extent, hallmarks. On the one hand, as will be seen in plays such as *Médée, Horace,* and *Théodore,* Corneille kept a certain taste for brutality. On the other hand, *Clitandre* is already replete with those cameos of Cornelian expression, the brief passages that strike or spellbind, whose echoes remain long after the initial perception, and which every Frenchman knows by heart and loves to quote.

III *La Veuve*

With *La Veuve* Corneille returned to true comedy, though it must be clearly understood that in all of these plays laughter is evoked far less frequently than sophisticated smiles. *La Veuve*'s resemblance to *Mélite*, however, goes well beyond that broad trait. As Corneille himself acknowledged, both in inspiration and in plot, this, his third play, owed much to the first. Sensing that the public was growing tired of the type of play exemplified by *Clitandre*, Corneille returned to comedy which to him had less to do with laughter than with "a portrayal of our actions and of our speeches." The plot, as can be seen from Corneille's own *argument*, is not unlike that of *Mélite*: "Alcidon, in love with Clarice, widow of Alcandre and mistress of Philiste, his good friend, fearing that the latter notice this love, feigns to love Philiste's sister Doris who, however, is not taken in by the stratagem and consents to marry Florange, as proposed by her mother. The false friend, under the pretext of avenging the insult that this newly proposed union is to him, gets Celidan to agree to kidnap Clarice and to bring her to his castle. Philiste, taken in by the false resentment of his friend, breaks up the proposed union with Florange, upon which Celidan tries to convince Alcidon to go back to Doris and to give Clarice back to her lover. Unsuccessful in his persuasion, he suspects an act of treachery and, deceptive in turn, gets the truth out of Clarice's nurse (who had been a willing accomplice of Alcidon) and, turning against the traitor, he brings Clarice back to Philiste and obtains Doris in return."

The parallel of structure is obvious, as are the literary commonplaces already found in the previous places (character of the Nurse, the betrayed betrayer, truth not being truth, and so on).[6] There are, however, some major steps forward insofar as the dramatic canon of Corneille is concerned. Whereas the first two plays were very loosely knit and had little unity of action (to all intents and purposes, the first love problem is settled at the end of Act I of each of the first two plays), *La Veuve* shows a determined effort on Corneille's part to cope with the problem. It is true that there are two actions, but they are properly connected. The first three acts are fairly well linked with only a slight difficulty in the last two. Still, we are a long way from Racine's concept, as enunciated in the preface to *Bérénice*, of a plot involving a minimal action taking place in a single locale in a few hours. For the unity of time Corneille chose to compromise, allowing one act a day. As for the locale, there is no indication whatsoever in the original edition, and, ten years later (1644), Corneille clarified the situation but slightly by adding that the action took place "in Paris."

Another aspect of the unity of action deserves comment. Not only is the plot more unified but the style of the entire play is closely linked with the dramatic development. Long speeches that have little to recommend them outside of their undeniable lyrical qualities and that advance neither action nor character of development are far less frequent than in the two previous plays, resulting in a greater sense of continuity in *La Veuve*. As Robert Nelson has suggested, "*Mélite* was a body of lyrics and *Clitandre* a tone poem. *La Veuve* is much more of an action." [7] This new awareness undoubtedly had much to do with the fact that *La Veuve* underwent relatively few changes in later editions, most of them involving the quality of the vocabulary, the propriety of certain expressions or manners—in other words, changes made naturally necessary by evolutionary processes in the realm of language and behavior.

This new awareness is also visible in Corneille's handling of the characters. Perhaps the most important scene of the play, as far as the study of the development of Corneille's psychological insight is concerned, is the one in which Clarice declares her feelings for Philiste (II, 4). In order to get the bashful swain to declare his own feelings, she goes as far as she can without violating the laws of propriety in a sense that is a masterpiece of delicacy and of psychological realism, a perfect wedding of preciosity and profundity. The author's insight is further demonstrated in the way he has the two lovers address each other. The first time they meet (I, 5) she uses the familiar *tu* while he uses the more polite *vous*. The next meeting occurs while the Nurse is present (II, 4), and so both use *vous* until Philiste dares declare his love openly, at which point Clarice, sure of herself, switches triumphantly to *tu* in a speech that also includes the then bold epithet "my Philiste." They do not see each other again on stage until V, 7, and by then Philiste is so torn between sorrow and joy, so insecure—can he believe his fortune? Does she really love him? —that he still insists on the more formal address while Clarice, sure of his love—"Do you see any signs of doubt in me concerning your love?" (1814)—never stops using *tu*. Of course, there are many reasons for this difference in expression. Clarice is a widow, that is to say a woman of a certain experience and knowledge, and so it is proper and natural that she display greater maturity, certainty, and even boldness. Her advantage in this respect is made greater by the fact that in social standing she is slightly above her suitor, if not enough to cause a scandal and make a union unbelievable, at least enough to make him doubt his good fortune. In *Mélite,* there had also been a *tutoiement,* a use of the familiar *tu,* a momentary lapse by Mélite immediately taken up by Tircis made sufficiently bold by it to ask for more tangible rewards. By 1648, however, Corneille considered this move too improper, and Tirsis, like his creator, learned how to keep his passion in check and to use the polite form of address under all circumstances. Clarice did not have to suffer from this unjust fettering, undoubtedly because Corneille felt that the ground had been well laid for her *tutoiement.* There is little doubt that much of *La Veuve*'s success was due to these flashes of psychological brilliance which are demonstrated not only in the above display of finesse but also in the creation of the many cameos that dot the play. Unfortunately, these are but oases, for Corneille had not yet learned to maintain the quality of his insight or his expression. Nevertheless, they give a very good indication of things to come.

IV *La Galerie du Palais*

The sub-titles of Corneille's early plays—*The False Letters* for *Mélite, Innocence Delivered* for *Clitandre, The Traitor Betrayed* for *La Veuve,* and now *The Rival Friend* for *La Galerie du Palais* —are always more indicative of the content of the plays than the titles themselves, and so it is indeed ironic that any mention of *amie rivale* is dropped from all the editions of the play as of 1644. As a matter of fact, the subtitle of this play, as of all the previous ones, should have been *The Dissimilations,* with an emphasis on the plural.

The plot, for once, is relatively simple: Célidée and Lysandre are about to be engaged while Dorimant loves Hippolyte who, in turn, secretly loves Lysandre. Célidée suddenly begins to yearn for Dorimant, making it a nearly perfect quadrangle. Taking advantage of this new infatuation Hippolyte suggests that her friend Célidée put Lysandre to the test by feigning indifference. Paid by Hippolyte, Lysandre's servant advises Lysandre to pretend to court Hippolyte to make Célidée jealous, but he is too righteous to keep up such a sham. In fact, both male leads are so steadfast in their virtue and love that the inevitable is brought about, the union of Célidée with Lysandre and of Hippolyte with Dorimant.

After the success of *La Veuve* it was to be expected that Corneille would keep many of the features of that play for his next venture, and indeed he did, improving on several of them. He continued, for instance, in the portrayal of life as the mainstay of comedy. As the title of the play indicates, the locale of the play is real, and realistically described. Other authors had previously described shops, or merchants, or the language of the lower classes, but never had the French stage seen all of these elements combined, and so well. The descriptions and illustrations of the speech, the mentality, and the general behavior of the shopkeepers; the incisive portrayal of types such as the cowardly swashbucklers—changed in later editions to rogues, attacking a passerby; the delightful commentaries on tastes ranging from clothes to literature; the description of a rowdy theater crowd (at the rival Hôtel de Bourgogne, of course)—all these now, for the first time, were introduced not as colorless background but as a vivid part of the play itself.

Like *La Veuve*, *La Galerie* is a step away from tragicomedy and its ploys. While there is little frank laughter, and while there are many changes of fortune, there is never any danger of seeing the plays lapse into the maudlin melodrama of tragicomedy. Overexcitement and excessive adventures are carefully avoided, there being but one duel, a common event in those days. The language is quite simple, even in scenes of precious debate, and the unforeseen turns of event allow for a multiplicity of tone quite becoming a comedy. The only strong derogations to this otherwise favorable picture of the physical makeup of the play are the facts that the characters have little relief and the unity of time is still not too well applied, Corneille again allowing five days for the action to take place.

Of primary interest in *La Galerie du Palais* are some major innovations. There are four principals, paired off, with no "outside agitator." Whatever changes of fortune occur do so, not because of external forces, but because of the stengths and weaknesses of the characters themselves. As Philip Koch points out, if there is to be any treachery, it "must come from one of the four principal lovers." [8] By the same token, there is no outside reconciler either, and so if the problem is from within, so is the solution, the former coming from the fickleness (Célidée) or the treachery (Hippolyte) of the women, the latter from the righteousness and willingness to act of the men. This "interiorization" of the action is of paramount importance to the comprehension of the evolutionary pattern of Corneille's dramatic technique. While secondary characters will continue to abound in his plays, their effect on the central action of the play will never again be of any consequence.

Perhaps of greatest interest is a concept of love destined to play a major role in later works and first introduced in *La Galerie*—though in the mouth of an insincere lover—namely, the concept of the importance of merit and esteem in the birth of love. When Lysandre, at the end of III, 6, claims that love as a blind passion is a thing of the past and that merit perceived intellectually gives rise to passion (916–18), he is not mocking a concept that later tragic heroes will exemplify. He, like so many comic antiheroes, believes that in matters of love, fraud is legitimate, whereas a Rodrigue will tell his father that there is but one honor, be it in love or in battle. But, and this is of paramount importance, Lysandre is a hypocrite, not an autohypocrite, and his statement is for public consumption, not to fool himself. He is, at the time of the utterance, not parodying but stating a valid concept, though he has not the slightest intention of fulfilling its promise.

V *La Suivante* [9]

Late in life, Corneille stated that basically all his comedies had been predicated on a single theme: two young people in love, separated for a while, then reunited. Of all the plays examined so far, *La Suivante* is probably the one that would suffer least from such an oversimplification. To be sure, a plot synopsis could easily be made as long as the play, because this is basically a comedy of errors, and if each one of these errors were to be related it would be a long synopsis indeed. Nevertheless, the story can be told quite simply. Fundamentally, there are two sets of characters: on the one hand Géraste, his daughter Daphnis, and her lover Florame; on the other, Théante, also in love with Daphnis, and the latter's *suivante*, Amarante. The first trio is fundamentally in agreement since Géraste wants the union of the other two, who love each other. The difficulties are introduced by the scheming pair, Théante and Amarante. After numerous misunderstandings, the true lovers are united while the schemers are not, the play ending with a bitter tirade by Amarante whose ambition has been thwarted. This last tirade, in alexandrine quatrains, shows her to be completely bewildered by all the misunderstandings, quid pro quos, and lies.

Outwardly, this is the most regular of the plays studied so far, with few innovations or surprises. The leading role is given for the first time to an attendant, but the Nurse as an old standby has already been replaced by a *suivante* in *La Galerie*. There is only one other innovation, one that will be of utmost importance in subsequent plays, and Robert Nelson has capsulized it to perfection: "The soliloquies do not merely recapitulate events or remind us of a character's role in a rapidly developing action, but serve rather to develop the character himself." [10] That is indeed a step forward, as are a rigorously maintained balance between the acts (each one of which has 340 lines) and the strictly enforced unities, though the unity of action is forced by the presence of some lengthy episodes that keep the interest from being properly sustained.

In our days, it is fashionable to speak of "antiheroes," comic or other. The term could very properly be applied to the protagonists of this play in which supposedly "honest" people act out of the worst of intentions. Whereas in previous comedies men's enterprises were either prompted by good intentions or were doomed to failure, here they are prompted by bad intentions and succeed. In an effort to simplify the plot, I have categorized the protagonists in such a way as to possibly suggest that only two of them were treacherous, but that is not quite so. Deception is not entirely limited to Amarante and Théante since both young men enter the house of Géraste under the pretext of courting Amarante.

PIERRE CORNEILLE

This simultaneous seduction of the mistress and the servant is a commonplace that can be traced as far back as Ovid's *Art of Love,* and as Clindor of *L'Illusion comique* will say, "Love and marriage use different methods" (789). Théante, confessing his feelings to a friend who will only too readily betray him to his rival, puts it equally well: "However attractive she may be, she is only a servant, and my ambition is stronger than my love" (9–12). It is this calculating cold realism that bewilders Amarante more than anything else, and it is particularly the misfortune of pretty but poor women betrayed by greedy men desiring wealthy wives that she bemoans. In short, we are right back to the basic question of honor in love. In that sense, Florame is no better than Théante, and keeping this in mind one reaches the inevitable conclusion that, while Amarante is a schemer, to be sure, she is a defensive one, as she is more victim—or even tool—than sinister plotter. Once more, a comedy ends, leaving the reader with the mixed feelings that perforce result from the perversion of the old axiom into "all is fair in the war of love."

VI *La Place Royalle*

The mood at the end of *La Suivante* is, if anything, amplified in the following play, *La Place Royalle*. Except for a few lighthearted moments, the humor of this play is grating. Even the plot gives an indication of the indistinct nature of the play: Angélique and Alidor are in love, but he wants to break with her in order to assert his freedom, and tries to "give" her to his friend Cléandre. Angélique receives a letter supposedly from Alidor to a rival, confronts him with it, and receives mocking insults in answer to her queries. Doraste, taking advantage of the rift, asks for the hand of Angélique. Considering his glory at stake Alidor asks for forgiveness so that Angélique might run away with him, planning to allow Cléandre to take his place at the last moment. This elopement, occurring at night, in the darkness Cléandre takes Phylis, sister of Doraste, by mistake. Horrified by all this, Angélique escapes to a cloister, a solution that satisfies Alidor who now feels free again.

Throughout the play Angélique is very close to being a tragic figure, mocked, tortured, finally seeking refuge in God, but not really sure or satisfied as a result of that decision. The reader may well ask himself whether Corneille, tired of the genre, had worked himself into a rut, or whether, perhaps, the play is nothing less than the logical outcome of the evolution we have witnessed so far, namely, if the comic protagonist insists on an immoral or amoral pursuit and succeeds, what is one to expect? Just as Alidor's ancestors are to be found in the previous plays, so are hints of the black comedy that develops here. In this respect, then, *La Place Royalle* offers nothing new to the reader. By the same token, while Alidor and Philis are marvelously drawn characters, beautifully delineated, Corneille had succeeded in doing that before, though the exact degree of such a success is debatable. The exterior realism—the Place Royale is today's Place des Vosges—is not new either to the author, and the unities are observed no better or worse than before. In what sense then does the play deserve attention? Its importance resides, in part at least, in the fact that the action is more than ever the result of inner forces, in this case the struggle between two feelings within the breast of the protagonist.

From the first line of the play, a rapid tempo is established, though this rapidity is often verbal, not involving the advancement of the plot or character development. Soon the attentive reader perceives that this breathless rush is indeed deceptive, and the play grinds to a teeth-gnashing end. But does all that matter? The plot is, as a matter of fact, well conceived, and the unity of action fairly well kept, but all that is nothing more than a framework for the real play, the inner struggle within Alidor, one whose ups and downs no doubt have much to do with the varying tempos of the "outer" play. In that respect there is a certain harmony between décor, subject, and characters which overrides all other considerations. Alidor is forever torn between a genuine love and an equally genuine, and eventually much stronger, desire for freedom which might easily be construed as a misguided sense of self-respect. He wants to love because he chooses to, not because of an obligation due to the lady's own attentions. He demands to be master of his love, not its slave (209–32). As Koch puts it,[11] Alidor is thus simultaneously the hero and the "*fourbe*," the protagonist and the antagonist. He strives to be extraordinary, to rise above social norms (209–10). Here, as in previous plays, the subtitle, "L'Amoureux extravagant" or the "Extragavant Lover," helps immensely in the understanding of what the play is all about. The word *extravagant*, in the Cotgrave dictionary

(1611), is defined as "astray, out of the way." Alidor, whatsoever his concept of self may be, is a comic antihero. Although he does not lack in will to act, he is quite incapable of doing anything about it, thus forever allowing the situation to backfire and turning any potential sympathy one might have for him into derision. He seeks freedom above all else, yet constantly depends on others, mostly on Angélique. Concerning his relationship with the latter, he does not even have the strength of character to abandon her, and must therefore behave so that she will reject him. It is precisely this divorce between the concept he has of himself and his actual being that makes Alidor comic and, in an anachronistic way, a parody of the real Cornelian hero.[12] Alidor's "extravagance" is further demonstrated by his lack of a true sense of values, and therefore of a goal. The few values that he manages to enunciate are negative, as if the author had wished to warn us against these before proposing more valid ones. Wandering aimlessly Alidor thus stumbles into victory, unaware not only of the misery he has created for others, but also of the emptiness of what seems a triumph to him, but is nothing more than utter failure. It is precisely what he states that "henceforth I live, since I live for myself" (1579), that one feels like asking him "why?" What is this *moy* for which he so wants to live? The best that can be said for it, the most that he can guarantee for himself at the time of that last tirade is that he will never again be caught or hurt by love. Poor victory indeed, and not much of a career. It may well be, as Octave Nadal has suggested, that Alidor "announces Rodrigue," [13] but hardly in any positive manner.

VII   *L'Illusion comique*

With *La Place Royalle,* Corneille must have felt that he had exhausted the vein that had brought him great fame and some fortune and he turned to tragedy, a form that was enjoying a tremendous revival at the time. Still, he did not abandon comedy entirely, and within months of the creation of *Médée,* in the summer of 1635, *L'Illusion comique* was performed for the first time.[14] Insofar as the plot and the characters are concerned, *L'Illusion* is a radical departure from the previous plays.

Pridamant, a good burgher, alienated his son Clindor through excessive severity ten years previously. To obtain some news of him, he consults the magician Alcandre who proposes to show him, magically, some of his son's many adventures. As the play within the play begins, we see Clindor—who has had many adventures and jobs in the ten years—in the employ of a swashbuckling Matamore. Both love Isabelle who is further admired by Adraste, while Lise, the maid of Isabelle, loves Clindor. While Matamore boasts of imaginary exploits and flees at the slightest danger, Clindor and Isabelle confess their love to each other. Jealous, Adraste fights Clindor who wounds him and is cast in jail for it. He is about to be condemned to death, but Lise conspires to allow him to escape by offering herself to the jailer, who loves her. The four are about to escape when the magician interrupts his evocation to show something even more startling to Pridamant. As the last act begins we see Clindor, who has obviously forsaken Isabelle, courting a princess whose husband sends men to kill Clindor for his boldness. But this tragic scene is an illusion in every way: we have just been allowed to witness a play within the play within the play, in that Clindor and Isabelle, after their successful escape, had joined a troupe of actors and were merely performing this fragment of tragedy. Pridamant, impressed by his son's success, goes to join him in Paris.

As can readily be seen from this plot summary, *L'Illusion* is indeed a departure from the vein previously mined by Corneille. This departure, however, concerns only the story and the main characters, for in theme, *L'Illusion* is the culmination, not the rejection, of the earlier plays. Until this play Corneille had shown a deftly controlled verve which he now let loose in what Garapon had called "verbal fantasy," concentrated in the person of Matamore, the *miles gloriosus* of antiquity, brilliantly revived by Corneille. More important still is the idea, not that Matamore lives in a world of fantasy (in that his exploits are imaginary), but that his world is literally an illusion which is not to be taken seriously. *L'Illusion* not only contains a very eloquent apology for the theater—culminating in the scene that sends father to rejoin son—but it is the embodiment of Corneille's dicta. The people creating illusions, be they magicians or actors, and illusion itself are the real heroes of the play. Appearances forever preempt reality, and Alcandre is not unlike Corneille himself in that respect. One might well ask why Alcandre does not, as requested, satisfy the father by giving him news of his son in a straightforward manner. If he did, of course, there would be no play, but the real reason is more complex for, as Clifton Cherpack points out, Alcandre, like a playwright, is compelled by the very presence of a captive audience to "demonstrate his talents." [15] For all their supposedly realistic descriptions, the early plays revolve around the reality-fantasy dichotomy. At the end of *L'Illusion* the realistic father who, by his own confession, had been too harsh with his son, runs to escape into that son's newly found never-never world.

Nor is this the only way in which *L'Illusion* caps off the early plays of Corneille. The Machiavellian lover, not averse to wooing both servant and mistress, is again found in Clindor, courting both Isabelle and Lise. The father cast in the role of benevolent despot because of his desire to impose a reasoned will on rebellious lovers is the remorseful spectator of his son's adventures. In *La Place Royalle* a young man was willing to sacrifice his love for the sake of an inner peace. In *L'Illusion* the young people constantly remind the older "spectators" that such is precisely their quest. Isabelle intends to be absolute mistress of her destiny (906, 515-16, and so on) in her search for "happiness and inner calm" (664). The father realizes soon enough that when he opposed his paternal authority to his son's quest for freedom (26), he invited disaster. But most important is the idea, implicit in all the plays from *Mélite* to *La Place Royalle*, explicit here, that all the world is a stage. *L'Illusion comique* deserves its complete title not only in that it ends well, but because "illusion" is the basic characteristic of "comedy," a word frequently used in the seventeenth century in its broader sense, denoting "drama" or "theater." *L'Illusion comique* is, in fact, the triumph of theatrical illusion.

If these early plays had to be reduced to one or two central ideas or themes, it would have to be the very Baroque ones of instability and illusion. All the titles or subtitles, from *Les Fausses lettres* to *L'Illusion comique* bear witness to that. The world of these plays is, in the words of *La Veuve*'s Philiste, chaotic beyond remedy (919-20), and is ruled by fickle fate with only "uneven order" (*L'Illusion*, 1725-28). To make matters worse, men contribute to this chaos, so that nothing is really as it seems: letters are not letters, friends are foes, confidants are spies, reality is a dream, and dreams are real. Small wonder then that many characters, like Philis of *La Place Royalle*, reject fidelity as a "vanity" (47-48), believing that steadfastness in an unstable world can only lead to unhappiness. Freedom, to these characters, is thus not a goal sought for its intrinsic value, or a sine qua non of self-attainment, but a protective wall saving the "hero" from involvement. Nowhere is this more evident than in *La Place Royalle* where the walls that imprison Angélique not only protect her from an unreliable world but also save Alidor from a dreaded servitude; it is no less apparent in *L'Illusion,* where all escape into the make-believe world of the theater. It is this world of marionettes on a treadmill that Médée, the first truly tragic heroine of Corneille, rejected, because she was essentially a stranger in it, and by so doing gave the theater audience of 1635 a preview of what we have come to call Cornelian drama.

CHAPTER 3

The Heroic Lie

I *Tragedy and Tragicness*

CORNEILLE'S greatest tragedies are frequently denigrated by Anglo-Saxon readers who will not, or cannot, accept some of the very basic concepts on which these plays are predicated. In the introduction of his edition of *Polyeucte* and *Le Menteur*, Georges May alludes to that problem when he states that "It is hardly surprising . . . that a play like *Polyeucte*—labeled in 1660 *tragédie chrétienne*—should appear to us neither tragic nor Christian." He continues, adding that "*Polyeucte* cannot be considered a tragedy if we define tragedy in forms of *Œdipus-Rex*, *Othello*, or *Phèdre*. Yet as a play, *Polyeucte* does fit the less metaphysical concept of tragedy prevalent in mid-seventeenth-century France: a serious five-act play, written in an elevated style and in alexandrines; with protagonists of noble blood engaged in a significant action, at least one of whom loses his life by the time the play ends.[1] To be sure, *Polyeucte* is not *Othello*, but Mr. May's statement nevertheless begs for comment. For one thing, Racine's *Esther* is in three acts, La Serre's popular tragedies are all in the most pedestrian prose, and no one dies in *Bérénice*. For another, Aristotle had said that the passions depicted on stage should evoke terror and pity; most of the critics at the beginning of the seventeenth century translated that statement as meaning horror and pity, but by mid-century there was near-unanimity in the idea that pity had to take precedence over fear or any other feeling, and Racine, in the preface to *Bérénice*, categorically rejected the need for blood and death, demanding only a "majestic sadness." Corneille deviated even more radically from the Greek concept of tragedy, rejecting even the idea of pity as a necessary ingredient, witness his preface to *Nicomède*—or the play itself, allowing the pathos to spring from sheer admiration. In short, as did R. C. Knight, I see seventeenth-century tragedy as "a Form, which is a species of the genus Drama, and distinguished from Comedy still by the four points of Lanson, modified in only one particular: *historique ou légendaire, royale, élevée de style,* and if not *sanglante* of necessity . . . at least including that Peril on which Corneille founds his Unity of Action." [2]

This definition, however, is quite limited, since it concerns only form, a structure, and how can a structure be tragic? A linguistic difficulty compounds the problem: in English we have only one word, "tragedy," whereas the French have two, *tragédie* and *tragique.* If I may be allowed to use the expression "tragicness" to translate the latter, then the problem can clearly be posited as follows: tragedy is of the realm of literature, whereas tragicness is a dimension of human existence.[3] To the extent that the hero belongs to the form, he is easily definable; in Corneille, we invariably have a noble man occupied by noble deeds and coping with what might loosely be called his destiny. But beyond that, when he and the spectators are on the threshhold of the aforementioned human existence, the archetype perforce disappears.

The heroes of Corneille's tragedies are invariably engaged in the pursuit of a hidden reality, an ambition so exorbitant as to be doomed to defeat. This quest is always triggered by what Jean Starobinski has called an *éblouissement,*[4] a dazzlement. The drama of *Le Cid* does not really begin until Don Diègue asks the famous question: "Rodrigue, have you courage?" This is not only true of the great tragedies: in the very first scene of *Mélite* Tircis sees a lovely face and forgets everything else; Dorante, in *Le Menteur,* is dazzled by Paris, and in *La Suite du Menteur* by a mere portrait; and in *La Toison d'or* such a portrait manages to change an entire stage into a resplendent garden. When young Rodrigue is thus challenged by his father's question, when he is dazzled, there is no hesitation: "Anyone but my father would find out on the spot." Is this attempt to be dazzling in turn immediately successful? No. Rodrigue, wishing to be dazzling, has donned a mask; he has set out to fulfill his own destiny and is condemned to strive to become that which, at that creative moment, he claims to be.

In Corneille, the hero, be he tragic or not, is merely appearing. For the tragic hero, this appearance is neither an image of a preexisting fact nor an out and out lie. He owes his sense of self to his birth. "In the greater number of plays, by far, the Cornelian *généreux* is noble and virtuous (Latin: *virtus,* manly as well as morally pure) in birth and in station and *thus* noble and virtuous in deed. His duty may be to himself, but his sense of self is derived, not forged. . . . The ethos is 'essentialist' rather than 'existentialist.'"[5] Rodrigue dons a mask, he plays a role, but it is an essential role, that is to say it is in the fulfillment of his destiny. He strives to become the mask, a mask that is nothing more than the realization of his capabilities. On the other hand Dorante, a comic hero, dons a mask that has no connection with his essence, and is thus laughable. From the very moment of dazzlement the Cornelian hero must, by his deeds, prove that his boast was not empty. He must become what he claimed to be. The essential hero can either succeed (Rodrigue) or fail owing to circumstances beyond his or her control (Chimène). The comic antihero, who has assumed a nonessential role, is doomed to be ridiculous (Matamore).

This essential position is at the basis of Cornelian tragicness. The individual, sacrificed by the mask on the altar of glory, and painfully aware of it, is the element that moves—be it by means of admiration or pity—and gives rise to tragicness. With few exceptions, the heroic mask leads the man into an impasse from which there is no exit. The issue is settled very early in the play, allowing our attention to focus exclusively on the admirable behavior of the hero confronting his hostile destiny. Long before Pascal, Corneille saw that man's grandeur resided in his facing that "cowardly foe" (*Médée,* 313), not as a matter of life or death, but of free choice and human dignity.[6]

II *Médée*

Médée is Corneille's first tragedy in name and in fact. It is certainly "historic or legendary, and royal," and there is no lack of blood by any standards. While the Senecan horror has been toned down somewhat, the story itself owes much to its Roman antecedent. As the play opens, Médée, who has killed her own brother and renounced all ties with kin and country for the sake of her love for Jason, is about to be supplanted by Créuse in Jason's heart and bed. At first Médée swears vengeance on all concerned but soon decides to limit her victims to two: Créuse and her plotting father Créon. The latter banishes Médée but forbids her to take along her children. Adding insult to injury,

Créuse demands that Médée personally bring her a beautiful robe which is Médée's last remnant of her former glory. In the meanwhile, Ægée, old king of Athens and rejected suitor of Créuse, tries to abduct her but is taken prisoner instead. Médée frees Ægée, who promises to avenge her and offers the hospitality of Athens. She accepts only the latter, being already assured of a better and faster means of revenge: she has sent her robe to Créuse, but not before charging it with a fatal charm. When Créuse dons the robe, she is immediately consumed by a mysterious fire, as is her father, who tries to rescue her. While Créon hastens his own death with a dagger, Créuse agonizes slowly before the powerless Jason. Moments later Médée tells him that she has killed their children, and she departs in a flying chariot while Jason kills himself.

Médée is hardly an attractive heroine. As a result, critics have given short shrift to the play. One brands Médée as an inhuman megalomaniac, and two of France's best-selling school manuals devote each one sentence to the play, calling it a dismal failure in spite of a few beautiful lines. While no one can think of *Médée* as a great play, it does have some aspects interesting if only because they shed light on the development of Corneille's concept of tragedy. Seneca had been a harsh model, and Corneille, unlike some of his contemporaries, never relied on him again. To make the play more palatable to his time, Corneille eliminated most of the Senecan melodrama and the pity too deeply rooted in the physiological. As he later said in the *Discours du poème dramatique*, the heroine's actions may be detestable but their source is admirable. In such a play the important consideration is one of focus, for, while the play is undeniably a tragedy, it may not always be tragic in all of its aspects.

The style of the play gives an important hint: in the opening scene of the play, we are in the presence of two impertinent fops discoursing in a tone suitable only to a comedy or, in modern times, an operetta. As soon as Médée herself appears, the tone changes, an early indication of her isolation in this whipped-cream world.[7] Her entrance is generally regarded as one of Corneille's great achievements, a startling contrast to the first three scenes, revealing her not only to be a sorceress among men but also a tragic figure in a world of marionettes.

Some critics have suggested that this stylistic disparity was

necessary for the public to immediately sympathize with Médée, but such an argument is open to question: why should Jason repel us simply because he moves in an aura more suitable to comedy than tragedy? It would seem that Bernard Dort came much closer to the truth when he said that the Cornelian hero is alone in a world whose reality is only spectral.[8]

In the person of Médée we have two beings, one human, the other superhuman, and the latter cannot bear the reviling to which the former is subjected. Médée, like all the tragic figures that Corneille will create, is thus doing her utmost in a struggle to preserve the integrity of her self. Until now she has given up everything for a Jason who always tries to arrange things and fails in his every effort to appear heroic or virtuous. Using her supernatural powers, she had completely sublimated her life to his. This is precisely what makes his betrayal so unforgivable and so stupid: "Can he leave me after so much kindness? Dare he leave me after such crimes?" she says, reproaching him for having a short memory as well as a fickle heart (229–32). It is this stupidity that makes so many of the characters seem ludicrous: they are fully aware of Médée's powers, yet fail to heed her warnings. In some ways, they are dazzled by her powers; in other ways, they seem totally unresponsive, even seeking to assert an unworthy autonomy, an ambivalence that is not without its comic side. Thus Créon pompously confronts Médée—"Can you, without fear, endure my presence?" (374)—only to hide behind his soldiers at her first threatening gesture.

Créuse is equally ludicrous in her desire for Médée's garment, equating it with her feelings for Jason (588–92), and both monarchs are silly mediocrities with Ægée compounding the fault by also being a senile lover and an impotent hero. In the company of such caricatures, Médée finds herself strangely "powerless" (315). *Médée* is thus the first of a long line of plays in which heroism is pitted against Machiavellianism. Jason, who accommodates his heart to his affairs (30), is as vile as Créon (387–96), and both are equally transparent in their hypocrisy. To find values beyond this human farce, Médée has but one choice. When her servant asks her what she will have left in her hour of defeat, she answers proudly: "Myself. Myself, I say, and that's enough" (320–21). And yet this early, difficult decision is far from final at that point, and much vacillation will have to follow despite the dramatic declaration that accompanies that "myself":

> Yes, you see in me alone both the steel and the fire,
> Both the earth and the sea, both Hell and the Heavens,
> Both the scepter of the kings, and the lightning of the Gods.
>
> (322–24)

But she is not yet as self-sufficient as the declaration implies because of her love for Jason. Her next confrontation with the unfaithful one begins with her pleas which only Jason's cynicism changes to threats: "Who will resist me if I want to punish you?" (896). Little by little Médée becomes aware of her failure. As a woman, she has failed to hold her man; as a sorceress, she has failed to awe. The result of realization is a quasi-Sartrian anguish from which she can tear herself only by eradicating the present and its absurdity: "Demain, je suis Médée." Note the tense: "Tomorrow, I *am* Médée" (1251). Her desire for revenge is real, but not nearly as strong as this need to reestablish her identity. As Paul Bénichou has so aptly put it, there is an inner need pushing the hero or heroine faced with defeat to seek the ideal. To prevent humiliation there must be a "desolidarization" from the hostile universe, one which Médée accepts only as of line 1251. This "desolidarization" is made all the more obvious by her attitude toward her powers over the world of mortals: if she accepts Ægée's offer for shelter, it is not because she has anything to fear from her foes but because she is tired of fighting them with her magic (1257–64).

The last act is nothing more nor less than the logical resolution of Médée's problem. However painful it may be, the murder of her children has become a fatal necessity. These murders are undoubtedly sins against nature for, as Médée explains it, they save the children from a fate worse than death: the transmitted shame of their father and the fateful legacy that would inevitably accompany it.[9] Médée sacrifices, in that sense, not her natural maternal feelings as much as the obvious for the higher and more fundamental. Her act is, for herself and her children, an escape from the world of Jason and Créon. As she puts it to Jason, she kills them to "drown, in their blood, the remnants of our love," to remove once and for all the witnesses of his faithlessness (1542–48).

In fact, there is no need to distinguish between motives of revenge and self-attainment, for it is by regaining her purity that Médée attains her vengeance. Until that climactic moment, she has been frustrated in her every effort. Now it is Jason's turn to be thwarted because his hopes for happiness and power died with Créuse. Rejecting suicide, he decides to avenge her instead. First he will kill his children, but before he can end his wavering, Médée preempts that effort. He then decides to kill her, only to find her disappearing in a chariot drawn by supernatural monsters which simultaneously removes her from her sorrows and his sight (1582). Jason's last words of bravado—"Nothing is impossible to one who knows how to love well" (1609)—quickly give way to the realization that any further efforts on his part would only heighten Médée's triumph. In that respect, his suicide is completely superfluous, and Médée is not even present at it. But this ending of the play is not as anticlimactic as some critics have suggested. *Médée* is a very logical play, one in which two distinct types— Médée on the one hand; Jason, Créuse, Créon, and Ægée on the other—move on two distinct levels, never able to communicate. Jason's gratuitous suicide is but the consecration of that notion.

III *Le Cid*

Having had but a partial success with Seneca, Corneille made a radical change, finding his inspiration in a contemporary work, de Castro's *Mocedades del Cid* (1621). The true genius of Corneille is made manifest in every aspect of the adaptation from the Spanish model which is a long, rambling dramatic poem in which the tragic rubs elbows with the comic, the trivial with the epic, and the tasteless with the sublime. Corneille must have been immediately responsive to the exaltation and grandiose proportions of de Castro's work, but he also had the finesse to see that precisely those aspects that had pleased the Spanish public would not please the French and that, consequently, many changes were necessary. He reduced the number of characters, eliminated the subplots, and toned down or removed anything that might have offended the tastes and demands for verisimilitude of the seventeenth-century French public.

Keeping the romanesque ideal and the flamboyant style of the original, imbuing his work with a youthful vigor that he was never again to attain, Corneille fashioned a play that took Paris by storm.

As Boileau put it, all Paris had for Rodrigue the eyes of Chimène. There is a variety of tone that still commands the admiration of critic and public alike: the drama of stichomythy, the pathos of *stances*, and the epic grandeur of the narrations all bespeak a freshness and spontaneity that bent the laws of drama to the needs of creative genius. The first audience of *Le Cid* viewed and heard an intelligent and logical debate, one laden with what Serge Douvrovsky was to call, more than three centuries later, heroes' dialectics, but one also that could move the staunchest heart to tears. This Romanesque ideal, reminiscent of a feodality that gave birth to the legend of the Cid and of the *précieux* novels so in vogue in the 1630's, is seen in the theme of contrary obligations simultaneously accepted by a hero that is central to the play.

The most important of all the changes operated by Corneille on his model, one that shows to what extent he was governed by his flair for the dramatic, is that he centered the entire play around that theme, drastically reducing the scope of the action. Although crowded by modern standards, the plot is sufficiently simple to allow all the attention to focus on the inner conflict of the main characters. One may or may not accept their ideals, but the psychological realism and coherent expression of these is undeniable, and that, in a nutshell, is what the play is all about.

Chimène and Rodrigue love each other; nothing seems to stand between them and a happy union, not even the Infante, the King's daughter in love with Rodrigue, or Don Sanche, who loves Chimène. However, a quarrel breaks out between Don Diègue and Count Gormas, the fathers of Rodrigue and Chimène, respectively. The Count insults and slaps his much older rival, who asks his son to save the family honor. Rodrigue challenges the Count and kills him, thus obliging Chimène to petition the King for retribution. The latter is all the more reluctant to grant this wish in that, in the meanwhile, Rodrigue has saved the realm from the attacking Moors. Persistent in her demands, Chimène obtains from the King permission to allow Don Sanche to champion her cause, but the King insists that there be no repetition of such a battle and that Chimène marry the victor. After the duel, Don Sanche appears and Chimène, believing him to be the winner, curses him and admits her love publicly. When the truth is revealed, namely that Rodrigue had won, had spared his rival, and had sent him to bring the glad news, the King decrees that with time Chimène will forget her grief and a union will again be possible.

Throughout the play the emphasis, somewhat toned down in later versions, is on the "young lovers," as they are called in the second scene. Chimène's anxiety is not unlike that of Shakespeare's Juliet, and the later versions of *Le Cid* emphasize that ominous tone that makes us beware of her idyllic dreams. There is but one initial question, will the lovers he united? After the first act that question is replaced by another: will such a union ever be possible again? From then on, Chimène consistently shows a greater understanding of the problems involved, a situation that has caused several critics to suggest that the play should really have been called "Chimène."

To better see this point, however, it is important to first determine the origin of the tragic situation, and for this, a closer look at Rodrigue is necessary. While the case of Médée is easy to isolate and to define, such is not the case with Rodrigue. In attempting to make herself into a human being, Médée had betrayed her heroic origins. Thus, she re-became herself by abandoning her human mask. Rodrigue is confronted with a situation that is the very opposite in its origin: his adventure starts with a mask which, although it does not deny his origins, is nevertheless a lie, however heroic it may be. This adventure begins when his father confronts him with the possibility of a glorious future: "Do you have any courage?" This question puts the young and untested son on the spot. He is dazzled, and only a lie can save him from shame. His reply is "worthy," as the father states, but a lie nevertheless, since it presupposes the existence of a valor not yet demonstrated by the young man who, as the count will state later on, has never been seen with a sword in hand. At this stage, the plot seems to announce itself as the quest of Rodrigue who will try, by his deeds, to "verify" his original presumption, to realize his heroic life. In other words, we are asked by the author to witness a metamorphosis Rodrigue—Cid, not to witness an uneven and uninteresting battle between love and duty. Médée's solitude began when she found herself again. That of Rodrigue begins with his realization of his mask. One of the most touching scenes of the play is the one in which Rodrigue becomes fully aware of this destiny, and no line consecrates it more than the one in which he echoes Chimène's "my generosity must equal yours" with the reluctant "your generosity must equal mine" (930, 946). At that point, the focus is shifted from Rodrigue to Chimène, from his quest to hers.

If *Le Cid* lacks unity, it is precisely because of this shift of emphasis from Rodrigue to Chimène. At the beginning of the play we are told of a relationship between two lovers based to a large extent on a sense of parity. When Rodrigue returns from having killed Chimène's father, the dazzling hero seems at first unaware of the fact that he has destroyed that delicate balance. It is now Chimène's turn to be dazzled, and to reestablish the parity she decides that her generosity must equal that of Rodrigue (930). This is not a simple question of honor: repeatedly, Chimène is told that no one expects her to be so steadfast in her quest for justice. However, as a matter of fact, Chimène is not interested in justice, but in proving to herself and to Rodrigue that she is as generous as he, for only his death will show her worthy of him (III, 4). This is why she cannot accept his help and why she can only wish for failure (984) without ever stopping her attempts on Rodrigue's life. Limited physically as a woman in a man's world, Chimène refuses to allow her conduct to be guided by these limitations. It is in this context that the role of the Infante is most readily explained: it is particularly when contrasted with the Infante's femininity that Chimène's intransigence is obvious. Whereas the Infante forever wavers, unsure of her ability to resist temptation, Chimène is always quite sure of the path to follow, however painful it may be. The Infante, to keep herself from "degenerating," withdraws; Chimène chooses to hate. More than anything else, the Infante witnesses "first the depth and sureness of Chimène's love for Rodrigue, and then the seriousness of her intent to be his equal in heroism." The Infante's quest for peace and tranquillity serves "as a frame of reference and as a focus for the most important thing in the play—the heroic love affair of Rodrigue and Chimène." [10] This does not mean that one of these two heroines is less aware of her duty than the other, but rather that they face this duty in quite different manners, with the result that while the Infante finds her much sought *repos*, Chimène is doomed to frustration and to forever living her heroic lie. However, it is important to put this attitude in a proper perspective. Like Corneille's later creation, Bérénice, Chimène sees that a sacrifice is necessary in order to save the unfortunate couple's love. The sacrifice of their happiness, of the physical possession of each other, is needed so that love itself can survive. Bérénice will simply say, "Let us be loved forever" (1702); Chimène, by her deeds, implies no less.

As the play's central concern is love and lovers, the accent is on youth. As was true in *Médée*, and will be true over and over again in later plays, the older people of *Le Cid* are anything but sympathetic. In the earliest version of the play the old people are painted with almost brutal strokes. But Corneille never changed one aspect of this group of characters: their inability to understand the young heroes or to enter into their world and see its superior values. The death of the Count, catastrophic to the lovers, results in a jubilant Don Diègue insisting that Rodrigue share his happiness (III, 6). When Rodrigue tells his father that, having lost everything for him, he feels that he has more than paid any debt that may have been due, the old man really shows his limitations: "We have but one honor, there are so many mistresses (1058). To such a statement there is but one answer: "An equal shame follows the cowardly soldier and the faithless lover" (1063–64). Here, simply stated, is the courtly ideal alluded to earlier, the simultaneous acceptance of contradictory obligations so familiar to readers of medieval romances. For Rodrigue, there can be no choice, no compromise of the ideal. There is no choice between love and honor, but the basic notion of a love-as-honor that motivates the hero to the point where no deed is too dangerous, no sacrifice too great for the sake of that love (963, 981–84, 1095–96, 558–64, and so forth). Honor, under these circumstances, does not stifle love, but forces it to transcend its material limitations. When first aware of the problem Rodrigue may hesitate (324), but he knows, and admits to himself soon enough, that in either case he must lose Chimène (340). This is why he can have no regrets (878), having accepted the only valid path, however painful it may be. By the same token, Chimène cannot blame him, but must now equal him, no matter what (929–30), a sentiment that Rodrigue reluctantly echoes a few lines later. As Charles Péguy put it, "Honor is a love, and love is yet an honor." That is the kind of love that outlasts life, though it may never be realized in life. It is also a love which, as in the days of Tristan and Isolde, is not understood by the lovers' elders.

One important question remains untouched: if the basic concern of *Le Cid* is a heroic love affair, how is the play to be classified? Antoine Adam agrees with the original appellation of tragicomedy, while André Stegmann prefers the later label of tragedy. Jean Rousset denies that either the heroes of the climate of the play—or any other play of Corneille—can be tragic,[11] and Robert Nelson calls the play a romance.[12] Which of the above is right? To answer that question, one must return to the problem of the lovers and to the solution that Corneille offers.

Following Rodrigue's first great deed, Chimène must not only avenge her father but do it without the help of Rodrigue (954–56) so that her generosity will equal his. Her duty is not opposed to love but born of it (915–32). The question then is not whether she will succeed in her quest (her fondest hope is to fail), since she is doomed to fail and knows it, but how she will keep to it. Her attitude, not her victory, concerns us. Her generosity lies in her repeated efforts, in her refusal to yield to the King's tempting entreaties. In that sense, the King is quite right when he tells Rodrigue to allow time and his valiance to work in his favor, for as long as both lovers continue to strive they will remain worthy and keep their love intact. In that transcendental sense there is indeed no tragedy, but this should not permit us to think of an eventual wedding, as so many critics have suggested. Chimène's last words are of refusal, and the continuing harangues of the King are just that: empty words. Corneille himself was quite explicit on this matter. Commenting, in the *Examen* of the play, on Chimène's final silence, he said, "I know very well that silence is usually considered as a sign of consent; but when kings speak, it is one of contradiction." Some twelve years later, in *Pulchérie*, he returned to the problem and gave the same solution, when he has the empress say:

Silences at court are political.
As soon as we speak, whoever consents, applauds,
And it is by being quiet that one contradicts. (1578–80)

If one can speak of an ambiguous ending for this play, such ambiguity does not reside in the meaning of Chimène's silence but in the attitude of the hero himself: will the Cid allow the reappearance of Rodrigue? After all, it would only be then that full consciousness, full lucidity would be reborn in him, and with it tragedy in all its force, a tragedy on a level with that exhibited by King Lear in his "O, let me not be mad, not mad, sweet heaven!" (I, 5). But such total lucidity is not to be found among the early Corneille heroes. They are doers, and lucidity, as Nietzsche so well stated, kills action: in order to act, we need illusion, and Rodrigue is no Hamlet as Chimène is no Ophelia, and so even that last shred of ambiguity can readily be dismissed.

IV *Horace*

In February 1637, while the quarrel of the *Cid* was still raging, Corneille, as a member of the "Five," contributed to the writing of *L'Aveugle de Smyrne*. However, since no one is even sure of the extent of Corneille's contribution—limited in all probability to the first act—it is of no help in elaborating Corneille's canon. In the meanwhile, Corneille's silence was far from sterile. This is proven not only by the quick succession of premieres but also by the close resemblance of the plays, in all of which we have the heroic conflict situated in the struggle between personal and public interest.

Sensing that rules were being well entrenched, that tragedy was taking over from tragicomedy, that Roman topics were all the rage (along with a quasi-pedantic care for historic accuracy), Corneille came through with *Horace,* his first contribution to a long string of Roman tragedies.

A war has broken out between Alba and Rome, two cities with strong historic ties. To limit the bloodshed, the two cities decide to each select three champions to fight it out, the fates of the cities depending on the outcome. Alba selects the three Curiace brothers while Rome chooses the three Horace brothers. Ironically, the ties that bind the two cities have an echo within these families, as Sabine, the sister of the Alban champions, is married to Young Horace, while Camille, the sister of the latter, is engaged to Young Curiace. As Old Horace awaits news of the battle, he is told that two of his sons have been killed and the third has fled. The old man is ready to execute the coward himself until he finds out that it was all a ruse whereby the surviving son fled only to separate the pursuing foes in order to kill them one by one. When the victor returns, his sister Camille curses him and provokes him into killing her. For this he is to be tried, but the King yields to everyone's pleas and merely demands that Horace submit to an expiatory ceremony.

Throughout the play a perfect orchestration is apparent. Fate has seen to it that two families, bound by the strongest ties, must destroy one another. The suspense is maintained by a series of unexpected yet completely logical events (the decision to abandon the general war for a more personal one, the choice of champions, the postponement, the seeming defeat of Rome followed by its victory, and so on), heightened by the revelations—in some of the most intense lines Corneille ever penned—of the inner conflicts of the characters. Structurally, Corneille is careful to constantly balance scenes (Sabine-Julie in scene 1, Camille-Julie in scene 2), events (the choice of Rome in II, 1; the choice of Alba in II, 2), and attitudes (Horace-Curiace, 502–3).

In *Horace* the youthful zest of *Le Cid* is gone, replaced by balance, power, and a highly developed sense of imagery. As a result moving metaphors, such as the first reference to the matricidal war (55–56), alternate with savagely terse ejaculations (332, 385, 502). The alexandrine, all too frequently monotonous in earlier authors, is fully exploited. The first line of the play is cut in two, the second half reinforcing the second line. Twelve lines later, Corneille allows the second hemistich of a line to contrast with the first, and before the end of that first scene (88, 94), he develops entire antitheses within the framework of single lines. There procedures are quite frequent, but by far the most beautifully structured alexandrines are those in which Corneille presents the very essence of the speaker's inner conflict, such as Sabine's "In one I am wife, in the other, daughter" (732), or Curiace's confession to Camille: "More I am your lover, less I am Curiace" (574). The terseness of some remarks should not be uniformly construed as brutality. Horace's "Alba has chosen you, I no longer know you" (502) is indeed as brutal as the speaker, but the immediate rejoinder, "I still know you, and that is what kills me" (503) is equally terse though profoundly human. Even rejoinders of a few syllables containing the distillation of an entire attitude or way of life—recall the "*Moi*" of Médée—are less brutal than pathetic. When Old Horace, told of his surviving son's flight before three foes, is asked what he expected him to do, his simple "Die" is more heart wrenching than shocking.

The unities, although generally well observed, still present some problems. Horace, like Rodrigue, has a very full day, though his deeds do not shake credulity as much as those of his predecessor.

To satisfy the unity of place, Corneille resorted to a common device of his times, the abstract though restricted locale, but several critics have pointed out that, in order to keep the action localized, the King had to judge Horace in his own house, an unlikely situation. The plot is carefully linked, but many critics have nevertheless seen a flaw in the way Corneille conformed to the demands for unity of action: as in *Le Cid*, the hero undergoes more than one trial; and these critics have therefore called *Horace* episodic, Sabine superfluous, and the trial anticlimactic. To better understand the necessity of either Sabine or the trial, it is necessary to differentiate between "plot" and "action" and to see how the diverse crises are organically linked by a multitude of ties, each one representative of a particular level of meaning. While Horace is rather uncomplicated, *Horace* is anything but that.

There is, first of all, something to which the audience of the 1640's must have been particularly responsive: the father torn between family and patriotic duty, and the son totally estranged from this duality, a youthful fanatic given over to the idea of state as his sister, equally incapable of duality, is given over to love. The basic issue, at that level, is whether or not personal tastes or even morality are to be put aside for national interests.[13] The King, by his verdict, seems to give an affirmative vote which confirms the "interiorized" one already cast by Horace. But that very vote demands a reexamination of the act that led to the trial, the murder (or execution) of Camille, so criticized by Corneille's contemporaries.

By accepting his lot, Horace assures not only his future, but that of Rome. Camille, in attacking him, attacks Rome as well. The trial is therefore not a separate action but the last of a logical sequence of events, each one rigorously tied to the preceding one, all subservient to a higher order, a metaphoric unity pervading all, which sees its beginning in the war and its fulfillment in the results of the trial. What strikes even the casual reader of *Horace* is the struggle—echo of the more personal one—on the far vaster level between Alba and Rome, between Rome's obligation to its past and Rome's grandiose plans for the future. The magnificent stylistic unity of the play resides precisely in the juxtaposition of these parallel oppositions. On this level of national policy, the right or wrong of Camille's death is not so much a matter of verdict as of execution: insofar as Camille attacked Rome, she deserved death, and her death was the result of a "reasonable" act. Alba had been doomed from the start (1639), and Camille, by refusing to celebrate the victory insulted not only Horace but also the gods. Her "impious" wish (1333) demanded an act of "justice" (1323). But—and is this not what differentiated the two fathers of *Le Cid?*—there must be an orderly chain of commands and a dispenser of justice. However reasonable and just the death of Camille may have been, Horace begins his defense by stipulating before the King that whatever he believes is law (1537). By assuming the role of the King, Horace committed a grave offense. By his confession, he allowed the King to consecrate the execution, thus permitting the reidentification of Horace with Rome.

But *Horace*, despite its political overtones, is far more than a mere political play. It is above all the tragedy of a young man.[14] To be sure, he is not the only character in the play. Whereas in *Médée* and *Le Cid* the stage was dominated by one or two characters, there is a far greater evenness in *Horace*. Yet all the characters except Horace seem to have but one purpose: to fully and clearly present the young hero whose personality, however unpleasant it may be, is the result, not the creator, of history. Given the role of Horace in Roman history, Corneille had no choice but to make him a quasi-monster. To make him live, he had to surround him with people of merit who could bring out the best— or the worst—in him.

Camille, Sabine, Horace, and Curiace are the members of a quartet so delicately balanced as to make each one indispensable. One cannot speak of teams but of several relationships, each one the representation of its own kind of duality. Thus Sabine and Camille, as women, must suffer in the world of men. On the other hand, Camille and Horace, as Romans, are far more fanatical than their Alban counterparts. Furthermore, matrimony and betrothals having done their part, the parallels are strengthened.

Whereas Horace is strangely monofaceted, Curiace is not. Equally aware of country, glory, honor, yet unwilling to allow these to rob him of his integrity and humanity, Curiace goes to a war in which he does not believe, sacrificing his freedom, but not his soul. "He keeps his dignity, his inner protest," willing to die, but never duped by blind and necessary patriotism.[15] A deeply human hero, he allows himself to be moved (503) but never shaken (478), his determination as strong as that of Horace (462–

78). Echoing Rodrigue, Curiace proclaims that there is room for both honor and Camille in his heart (264) while his conscience recognizes that it would be a "crime" to repudiate either (596). In time he is forced to betray that conscience by choosing. In so doing he is no doubt touching, but less so than his sister who keeps it intact. By choosing, Curiace does not remove the absurdity of the situation; he merely bows to it.

Not so Sabine. Although the seventeenth century admired this Cornelian creation, later critics have considered her superfluous. But she is of the utmost importance. First, there is the obvious matter of balance and structure. Thanks to her presence Horace finds in Curiace a brother-in-law, another self, whom he can fight with the same joy that he demonstrated in marrying Sabine (500). Furthermore, Sabine is necessary to offset not only Camille's proud individualism but also Curiace's capitulation. By refusing to accept either one of two unacceptable alternatives, she asserts the nobility of man pitted in battle against fate. Perpetuating her anguish, she bows to no contingency.[16] When she suggests to the two young warriors that one of them kill her and the other avenge her in order to make their task easier, she is not only savagely ironic; but by contrasting the integrity of her conscience with the barbaric notions of honor and glory of the men she is thoroughly tragic. To be sure, she knows that her horrible suggestion is unacceptable, but her purpose is to shake her interlocutors, not to solve their problems.[17] Her vision is that of an Ophelia, doomed, as she foresaw (647–53), to live alone in a Roman world and to embrace the victor of this fratricidal combat.

Like her brother, Camille is not satisfied with merely accepting her lot; she actively pursues it, resolved to "die of joy." She is as fanatical as Horace, though in quite another vein. Recalling Rodrigue, she considers the unfaithful lover a criminal (152, 156). Unable to marry a man who is either the master or the slave of Rome, she will, nonetheless, keep her love intact. When both her brother and her father deny her this right, she rebels against what she feels to be unjust tyranny (1197–98), affirming her self through her love, and by her death sullying the hated reputation of her brother, as her triumphant curse demanded (1293–94).

Horace is by no means a Cornelian ideal. From the very beginning of the play the author tells of a need for emotions and an expectation of troubled minds in even the most manly of heroes.

In that sense Horace falls quite short. Self-assured, monofaceted, Horace is as unyielding as he is unchanging. Like Rodrigue, he sees the need to constantly re-create himself, as he sees the need to attach this quest to a cause, to an ideal that transcends the ordinary values of individuals. Yet for him this involves no transformation; we are here in the presence of a fait accompli. As Rodrigue had found out through harsh experience, each heroic deed demands another. Horace foresees this readily (1555–63, 1571–72) and is not confident of always being up to the task. This is why, during the trial, he would be glad to die lest he fail (1580–84). Such a death would not constitute a surrender to justice, but to glory: "My immolation is to my glory, not to my sister" (1594). The nature of his crime, in his own eyes, is not the mere death of his sister. In that sense glory is as Descartes suggested in article 203 of the *Traité des passions de l'âme,* the reflection not only of inner satisfaction but also of public acclaim. By appealing to posterity to bear witness to his glory, Horace is willing to end his life at the moment of his greatest triumph, before any "degeneration" can occur. The King, motivated by reasons of state—as was the King of *Le Cid*—cannot allow Horace to die; however, he is forced to agree to Horace's summation of his position: "Your virtue raises your glory above your crime" (1760).

By ordering him to live, does the King extract another sacrifice from Horace? Not quite. Horace does not sacrifice himself to Rome, Horace *is* Rome, and if Rome wishes to free itself from its origins, Horace can do no less. Rodrigue rid himself of inner witnesses; Horace, like Médée, must rid himself of witnesses that are exterior although closely tied to his essence. As he states himself, Curiace is "another self" (444), a conscience as bothersome as Camille. For Rome to become Rome, for Horace to fully realize himself as a political figure and as an individual, the catharsis bemoaned by his entire world is an absolute necessity, and no one sees this better than the King himself: as Walter Albert has noted, "The king, by . . . proposing a new sacrifice to purify the sacifice which Horace has unwittingly made, also provides for that symbolic union which is the union of Alba and Rome." [18] In this context, the death of Camille can be viewed in a new light. Camille has refused to acknowledge the will of the gods who have decreed the supremacy of Rome. This leads Horace to forsake patience for reason (1319) and kill her, thus agreeing to be the instrument of the gods. His glorious sacrifice is in that lucid assumption of the crushing responsibility that, misunderstood by all, can lead only to solitude.

The misunderstanding of Young Horace is general, even involving his father to some extent. If Old Horace considers his son guilty, it is because he took justice in his own hands. The shame is on both children: on Camille for the thoughts she entertained; on her brother for the deed. In one respect he understands his son: private feelings must be subjugated to public weal. He does not however see, like his son, that this is precisely what made his son act as he did: Horace, through his deeds, is Rome. The extent of the misunderstanding can be seen in the varied ways in which the fratricide is interpreted. For Young Horace it was an act of "reason" (1319), Sabine saw it as the result of "anger" (1335), Old Horace as the initial reaction caused by his manliness (1648). The King conveniently dismisses a crime, which he considers inexcusable (1740), by virtue of state needs. Such a king, as Machiavellian as the one of *Le Cid*, cannot give Young Horace the fundamental understanding he needs.

The entire dramatic structure of the play revolves around this factor. The fate of two nations is at stake, and the fact that the problem is concentrated on two families and one day makes the atmosphere all the more heavy and oppressing. But, as André Stegmann has so clearly seen, Young Horace is the only one in the play to fully see the monstrous nature of the demands made of him by this inhuman fate.[19] In "blindly and joyfully accepting the glory" that is imposed (492), he finds the heroic solution that the others cannot. In that he is alone. Rodrigue, having found his heroic vocation, succeeded in infecting Chimène. Horace tries to do the same thing with all the protagonists in turn, and he fails. For this reason, he is far more alone—and tragic—than his predecessor. His sacrifices are also more painful: first Curiace, then his sister, and even closer "self." The tragedy perhaps is that he alone sees that the two immolations, autoimmolations at that, are so closely related. The same public that applauded the first condemns the second, an illogical dualism that leaves him completely bewildered.

V *Cinna*

Composed almost simultaneously with *Horace, Cinna ou la clémence d'Auguste* once more pits the individual against the state in a Roman setting. Emilie, whose father was killed by the emperor Auguste, has sworn vengeance, and has promised to marry Cinna if the latter accepts to be the instrument of her purpose. Just as Cinna triumphantly announces the plans of the conspiracy to Emilie, he and Maxime, a co-conspirator, are summoned by Auguste. Tired of ruling, the Emperor asks the two for their advice. Cinna, fearing that his prey will escape and thus rob him of Emilie, pleads for Auguste to stay on the throne, while Maxime suggests otherwise. After Auguste's departure Cinna explains his fears to Maxime who, jealous, sees to it that Cinna is betrayed to the Emperor. Auguste is torn between the need to punish and the desire to forgive, and his wife Livie advises clemency as a clever, Machiavellian gamble. In the meanwhile Emilie, having been informed of the betrayal, scorns Maxime. They are all summoned by Auguste who demonstrates his mastery over the situation by forgiving the conspirators.

More than any of its predecessors, this is a political play. It must be kept in mind that the *nu-pieds* rebellion started in Normandy in July 1639, that shortly thereafter the king's envoys were executing rebels left and right, and that in such a climate conspirators, both male and female, were as plentiful as in the more publicized Fronde that was to follow some years later and which Corneille undoubtedly foresaw. It would be wrong, however, to see in *Cinna* a reference to specific events or contemporaries. Emilie, as the embodiment of the adventuress, and Cinna, the *"Frondeur par galanterie,"* were readily recognized by all, not as neighbors, but as a common phenomenon. By the same token the political actuality of *Cinna* does not reside in a specific rebellion, past or predicted, but in Corneille's attempt to grasp the psychology and motives of conspirators as a whole. *Cinna*'s popularity, in terms of the total number of performances at the Comédie Française, is second only to that of *Le Cid* among the plays of Corneille. However, this rank is due almost exclusively to three periods: that of the debut, one between 1802 and 1820, and a third one between 1832 and 1850, all three periods of great political stress.[20]

The bulk of the testimony that has come down to us shows that *Cinna*'s original public was far more impressed by the lovers than by Auguste and his clemency. The ending was considered happy because the young couple surmounted its problems, not because Auguste transcended his. This is why they could view Cinna as an *"honnête homme"* and Emilie as an "adorable Fury," for if the moral ascendancy of Auguste is somehow relegated to a secondary level, the lovers can be viewed far more generously than if we focus on Auguste's regeneration. Corneille, as the title indicates, could not have disagreed with this viewpoint, although the subtitle and the very content of the last act more than justifies the predominant role given by most modern critics to the Emperor.

To place this question of changing focus in proper perspective, it is best to add some dimension to the major characters. Cinna, grandson of Pompey, has decided to kill Auguste to simultaneously rid Rome of a tyrant, avenge his grandfather, and assure his own glory. He solidifies this position by swearing to Emilie that he will carry out this plan that antedates his love (1628). Unfortunately, he is caught on the horns of a dilemma because he has repeatedly accepted favors from the Emperor. This is nothing new, but the character of the hero is. Cinna is undoubtedly young—though old enough to lead a conspiracy—but so were Rodrigue and Horace, and Cinna is not of their mettle. From the beginning Emilie foretells of a hero who will be worthy of her when he has fulfilled his pledge and liberated Rome. Yet Cinna, as of his first appearance, destroys this brilliant impression by his self-effacing tendency of making himself just another plotter. He speaks only of "their" courage, "their" memories, "their" hatred, and hardly remembers his own role in the political situation. There are times when he has a very hard time convincing anyone, including himself, of the fact that he is of the blood of the great Pompey. In the third scene he sees his role of conspirator as a glorious one; three acts later (III, 4) he has completely changed his mind. Such a change could be considered a simple matter of psychological evolution, of regeneration, but such is not the case. His original pledges (to ancestor, love, and himself) are due to youthful impetuosity, but this attitude is soon replaced by methodical reasoning. As did Rodrigue, he sees "perfidy" in repudiating either his vow to Emilie or his duty to Auguste (817–

18). Vacillating constantly, he cannot truly commit himself. He describes his followers in the most glowing terms but dares not protest when August refers to them as the lowest of rabble. He constantly proclaims his *"vertu,"* but when accused, he lies shamelessly (1477). Even some of his remorse may be said to be due to Auguste's promise of Emilie; in this promise, further proof of the Emperor's generosity and of Cinna's ingratitude, Cinna sees the possibility of obtaining Emilie without resorting to regicide. He is fundamentally a man caught in the resonance of his own rhetoric; too quick to engage himself in a path which he later finds to be totally unacceptable, but from which he cannot free himself, he must wait for Auguste's clemency to liberate him by allowing Emilie to retract her demand.

This contrast between the Cinna that is and the one that could be is particularly obvious in the last scene. Forced to wear the heroic mask, Cinna has been able to do little more than play a role, and at that, badly. While Auguste is "master of himself and of the universe," Cinna barely understands how his puppet strings are pulled by others. In fact, it is to Auguste that he owes his very freedom, for if he can at last put down the heavy burden of responsibility it is only because Auguste has invited him to live once again as his friend.

Emilie, though no less mediocre, is easier to understand. Moved exclusively by her emotions, be it her hatred (977) or her love (two emotions that vie constantly for supremacy in her heart), she struggles to master both in order to submit them to her sense of duty. The seventeenth century loved her, not because of her heroism, debatable at best, but because they saw in her a vibrant, passionate creature who, despite her emotions, could nevertheless see the truth when confronted with it. Her role is not of the same importance as that of the two men, but it is also least affected by the change in focus that has occurred since 1641, and, when all is said and done, one wonders whether that first public did not fall in love with the role rather than the character: in all dramatic literature there are few roles more difficult, more demanding than that of Emilie, a young lady who fluctuates repeatedly from anger to tenderness, from love to hatred, from youthful ejaculations to considered power (as in III, 4, where tenderness alternates with sarcasm and even violent hatred).

Opposed to this mediocrity is Auguste, readily aware of his

worth and to whom "Rome, Auguste, the State" are one and the same thing. Not that this is immediately apparent, since Auguste does not appear until the second act and then as a far from resolute monarch. It is only little by little that he finds himself, that, by his regeneration, he rises so as to transcend generosity itself. In this act Auguste appears as a man tired of ruling, personally yearning to be free of that burden, yet aware of his obligation to the state and ready to sacrifice his private desires. Insecure, he relies in turn on friends, whom he sees as they should be and as they could be (1517), and on the gods (1258). When he finally sees the light, he rejects the Machiavellian arguments of his wife who sees in clemency nothing more than a method of firming up the Emperor's popularity, freeing himself from all that surround him as he rises above them.

It is at this point that a new Cornelian concept springs forth. Until now there had been confrontations between the hero's quest for the absolute and the Machiavellian stand of the ruler. Now the ruler is the hero. Furthermore, there is no longer any question of solitude, at least not at the end. During the early stages of the play, the long political discussions present not only the original focus but the intellectual climate of the entire milieu. The arguments opposing the republic and the monarchy are merely echoes of the personal conflicts. There comes a point, however, when Auguste realizes that his former world, this world of political expediency, has disintegrated under his very eyes. Resorting then to his latent heroism, he declares himself master of himself, of the universe, because "I am, I want to be" (1697). The inverted progression is important here, betraying the intense struggle that takes place within him. Once that inner battle is won, Auguste is no longer alone. Following his ascension—which the gods dictated (1755), but in which he actively participated—he is not only master over his emotions and his universe but, even more apparently, over his fellow men. In the last line Auguste announces that he "has learned everything and wishes to forget everything," ending the play on a note already sounded in the subtitle. Prefiguring *Polyeucte* (on a secular level, to be sure), *Cinna* ends with a contagious regeneration in which Auguste, after his apotheosis, reaches out to save all those who once, like he, had sinned.

VI *Polyeucte*

Polyeucte shares much more than this final apotheosis with *Cinna*. Like its predecessor, this play has meant different things to different generations. There is no doubt that, to the contemporaries of Corneille, *Polyeucte* was primarily a drama of love in which religion interferes—at times unfortunately. Today, keeping in mind the fact that Corneille called it a "Christian tragedy," the French public views it as the illustration of the supremacy of divine love over its terrestrial counterpart.

Corneille was quite proud of the dramatic action of *Polyeucte*, which is relatively simple: Polyeucte, an Armenian prince, has just married Pauline, daughter of Félix, the Roman governor. Pauline has merely submitted, still harboring feelings for Sévère, a poor Roman rejected by her ambitious father, who went to seek death in the Persian wars after the rejection. Néarque, a friend of Polyeucte, tries to convert him to Christianity, not without some difficulty. To add to Pauline's worries, she has just had a dream in which she saw Sévère (whom she believed dead) covered with glory and Polyeucte killed in an assembly of Christians. Suddenly, the situation comes to a head: Sévère, far from dead, has covered himself with glory, has become the emperor's favorite, and is arriving in Armenia to participate in the ceremonies celebrating his recent victories. As they meet again for the first time, Pauline tells Sévère of her marriage and of her intent to remain true to her obligations and to her husband. During the celebration, Polyeucte, baptized at last, breaks the pagan idols. Arrested, he refuses to recant. Pauline, her feelings for her husband growing with every moment, enlists Sévère to plead for Polyeucte; but Félix, ever the politician and fearing a trick whereby Sévère, still smarting from the old rejection, might wish to make him compromise himself, sends Polyeucte to his death. Pauline announces that she is now a Christian too. To add insult to injury, Sévère roundly castigates Félix, who also converts.

The unity of action is here embodied to perfection, as the play begins with an exposition of conjugal love, almost petty and ludicrous in its banality, the pitch rising slowly but inexorably until the final Te Deum, the scenes between Pauline and Sévère and Pauline and Polyeucte merely stages on the steady ascension. Dramatically, the third act is the center of that ascension in more ways than one. On the most obvious level this is the act during which Polyeucte's fate is to be decided. More important, however, is the fact that it is during this act that the focus changes. Until now the danger run by Polyeucte was, as foreseen by his wife, of simply going to his death. The danger now is that, although he is imbued with grace, he will be unable to resist temptation in the form of his wife and all the earthly attractions she represents. As he readily admits to Pauline, he loves her more than his own life, though less than God (1280), and her presence is indeed a danger, capable of bringing him back to the pleasures of a life he thought he had forsworn (1105–4). This spiritual battle is engaged in only after he has armed himself with all the weapons in his mental arsenal (IV, 1 and 2). The battle itself (IV, 3), in the heat of which Pauline lapses from the formal *vous* to the more familiar *tu*, is all the more violent in that both protagonists are moved by love. Pauline is frightened by what she does not yet understand to be Grace, and wants to save Polyeucte from death. He, seeing the chance to convert her, speaks to her in favor of a higher, everlasting love. Although the battle has no resolution, the seeds are sown, and the rest of the act, and the early stages of the next, are but a dormant period preceding the imminent blossoming of Grace. What Polyeucte foresees in this fateful scene is not the replacement of Pauline by God, one love superseding another, but the conciliation of both through her salvation. The supreme irony of the ending of this scene (Polyeucte here is not only admirable in his stance, but to be pitied in his sorrow) is that Polyeucte abandons the quest, not knowing that victory is now inevitable. In renouncing this life and willing his wife to Sévère, Polyeucte has made the sort of sacrifice that commands Pauline's admiration and love. Consequently, Act V is truly what the French call *dénouement,* the unknotting.

Insofar as *Polyeucte* is a Christian play, it is a Cornelian novelty. Other aspects are more familiar: the same notions of glory and *honnêteté,* the same conflicts present in the previous plays are expounded here. In all modesty, Corneille could say in the 1660 *Examen* that, from the dramatic point of view, he had never put together a better play. Though its versification is not as majestic as that of the Roman plays, it is as flawless, and the content fittingly more touching. This can be explained by the less "Roman" topic, but there is an external factor perhaps not entirely foreign to the transformation. Between *Cinna* and *Polyeucte* Corneille had gotten married. Still on his honeymoon, so to say, he was obviously sensitive to certain aspects of love that had not touched him before. The prevailing mood of *Polyeucte* is emotional, not cerebral, and the play contains some of the most tender lines in all Corneille. Pauline is tender, whether alone or in some of her momentous duets, but so is Polyeucte, particularly in the earlier scenes. However, lest the play be made too autobiographical, it is well to realize that conjugal love is praised but that the truly touching scenes deal with another type of love altogether—that of Pauline and Sévère.[21]

As can readily be surmised, while some characters of *Polyeucte* are rather monofaceted, others are extremely complex. The characters form the widest spectrum of any seen so far, ranging from the fervent Christianity of Polyeucte to the calmer one of Néarque, from the virulent paganism of Stratonice (Pauline's confidante) to the enlightened one of Sévère, passing by the politically motivated one of Félix; in short, they range from the noblest to the most self-serving, from the truly *honnête* to the really *médiocre*.

It has often been suggested that the principal active character of this play is God. Without a doubt, the presence of Grace is manifest in Polyeucte and dictates his behavior and the outcome of the play. Before Grace is visited on him, Polyeucte is a very ordinary man. Willing to become Christian without deep commitment, rational, yet unwilling to go against the wishes of his wife, who fears for his life as a result of a dream, he is totally lacking this "perfect ardor" that Néarque describes (77). After baptism it is an entirely different story, although it would be wrong to see in him a harsh and unfeeling man. To be sure, there are moments that may lead to such conclusions, such as his final rejection of Félix's offer of safety (1647–79), but they should be seen as postures to fight what Jean Calvet has called the "uncommon tenderness" that threatened to lure the hero from his higher plane and to force the play into bourgeois melodrama.[22]

Whatever fervor animates Polyeucte is not from within, but from God. Furthermore, despite its elevated origin, it does not free Polyeucte from some very painful struggles in the exercise of his free will. During these struggles, the love theme is not opposed to the Christian one, but is essential and necessary to it. Polyeucte, in spite of what the more social characters around him may say, is as fully heroic as his dramatic predecessors, and that thanks to the lucidity of his vision during his travails. There is, however, a basic gulf that exists between Polyeucte and these predecessors. They concerned themselves with a worldly glory; Polyeucte does not, since he considers it his foe (1109). He does seek a glory, but a "noble, more beautiful" one, one that is immortal (1191–92). And yet a nagging problem remains, one to which the solution can be found only by seeing the role of the lesser protagonists, and that is the problem of Polyeucte's fundamental concepts. He may strive for heaven but only because there is a bigger and better glory there, a notion very difficult to reconcile with the presence of Grace. In his ascension he transcends all earthly matters, but his aims remain the full affirmation, not of God or of love for that God, but of his own integrity, bought at the rather low price of a sad and cruel life (1195). Polyeucte strikes one as being particularly sure of himself, almost arrogant, certainly proud. In that perspective Félix is far more "Christian," and his conversion—as shall be seen shortly—is a dramatic as well as theologic necessity.

Dramatically, the preëminence of Polyeucte cannot be disputed, but the fact remains that Pauline has nearly one-third of the total lines in the play, and her role demands that the actress demonstrate a maximum range. It is therefore easy to see why the seventeenth century was more involved with her than with Polyeucte, more with her love than with Grace. Her conversion, until the nineteenth century, was most frequently seen as an act of love rather than as the mystical experience that it is considered today.

Pauline has married Polyeucte out of filial duty, still harboring a vestige of love for Sévère. What mere marriage cannot do will be done by her growing feeling for her husband. Is this new feeling the same love as that which she had for Sévère? Not at the start. Passion does not yield to reason; rather, love-inclination yields to love-reason, the latter growing gradually until, completely devoid of affectation and unadulterated by womanly deceit, it forces Pauline into an emotional leap to pure love. It is difficult to say just which of the above forces are most operative when Pauline gives Sévère a lesson in duty and *honnêteté,* but there can be no doubt that when she refers to her husband as "My Polyeucte" (1336), when she can fearlessly refer to her love for Sévère as a thing of the past (1348), when, in the heat of her attempts to save Polyeucte from his error, she lapses from *vous* to *tu*, she is in love with him.

This is, of course, a dramatic necessity: the passage of Polyeucte from a terrestrial to a celestial love cannot touch a rational as much as an emotional person. Pauline's final leap to true love is the result of the shattering, dazzling conversation of Polyeucte. This moment does not come as a complete surprise. When Pauline first discovers that her husband has converted, she has the harshest words for the hated sect; but as she defends Polyeucte before Félix, she warms to the task, and his defense becomes a plea for all Christianity. The plea helps her to see the admirable traits of Polyeucte in particular, and of the Christians as a whole, an understanding necessary to her love and her salvation. Enlightened by her own rhetoric she sees that his sacrifice was all the more sublime because he did love her, and as his love commanded hers, now his Grace reflects on her. Baptized in his blood (1728), she in turn becomes "full of Grace" (1742), brought to the love of God by terrestrial love.

In every sense of the world, Félix is a mediocrity. Having ordered his daughter to reject a poor Sévère, he now demands that she see a powerful one. When she begs to be spared such a painful interview, he claims that she is too virtuous to succumb to her feelings, never realizing that what she fears is not a dishonorable lapse, but the very confrontation and struggle that offend any delicate soul. This imperviousness marks Félix as inferior to his daughter as Don Diègue was to his son.[23] Félix, ruled by his political astuteness, fails to understand Polyeucte or Pauline and is even bewildered by the all-pervasive Grace he cannot understand (1770-71). Sévère's anger has shown him the vanity of the values and things he cherished, but this is not much preparation for the ultimate conversion. Viewed on a human level, this conversion is ridiculous; yet as Jean Calvet states,[24] this is not a drama of humanity but of God and Grace, and God operates at whatever level man happens to be. This is why Félix hopes for the early conversion of Sévère (1809-10) and invites the Christians to a veritable Te Deum (1814).

If this is a drama of salvation, how is that Sévère, the perfect gentleman, does not convert? What is his role in the play? To be sure, he is the universal catalyst: by his presence he forces Pauline to face the old problem of her dormant love; his coming brings about the ceremony that allows Polyeucte to demonstrate his religious zeal; and his presence makes Félix afraid to pardon Polyeucte. There is more. He is totally mundane, a trait whose importance will be discussed shortly. Although truly generous, he never rises to the level of heroism. In language and deportment he is frequently precious, as in the early moments of his first meeting with Pauline. It is only later in that scene that Pauline forces him to face his generous nature, allowing the two—in one of the most touching duets in all Corneille—to overcome the situation, not with a victory of honor over love, but with a synthesis of the two that elevates the soul above both. In matters of religion, it is well to remember that in the original version Sévère thought public beliefs to be nothing more than politicians' tools to enslave the masses (IV, 6, following 1434). In later versions Corneille removed such seditious language, but not the thoughts. Sévère remains as a man willing to allow each man his own theology (1797–98) and anxious to see the coexistence of God and Caesar (1804).

This leads to a consideration not only of Sévère's real importance in the play, but of the true meaning of the entire play. Until now Corneille had demonstrated his very orthodox concepts of monarchy. Now, for the first time he shows himself as the champion of divine monarchy. As Michel Beaujour has so intelligently and rigorously pointed out, for there to be a Realm-of-God-on-Earth, it has to have solid foundations. Men like Sévère and Félix are at least as necessary for this as a selfishly irresponsible Polyeucte. Through the latter, Félix will be converted and Sévère will increase his already existing sympathy for the Christians. By telling Félix to serve his king *and* his God (1804), Sévère heralds the establishment of a coexistence. Félix the civil servant and Sévère the pagan—who must remain pagan if he is to keep his position at the court of Decius and thus protect the new Christian realm—thus profit from Polyeucte's excessive zeal. Once again, as in the previous plays, we see the excesses of the hero put to use by the ruler for the greater good of the establishment.[25]

VII *La Mort de Pompée*

The political preoccupations of Corneille, already demonstrated in *Médée*, and so masterfully treated in the tetralogy that followed, became the focal point of his next play, *La Mort de*

Pompée, in which the titular hero does not even appear and the attention focuses not on the characters but on the ideas and ideals they represent.

Pompée, who had established Ptolomée and Cléopatre on the throne of Egypt, has just been beaten by César and is now fleeing to Egypt. In the meantime, Ptolomée has succeeded in removing his sister from power. Fearing Pompée, Ptolomée listens to his advisors, particularly to Photin, and has Pompée assassinated as soon as he lands. César, however, had forgiven his foe, and on his arrival in pursuit, he harshly castigates Ptolomée who, driven by fear, plots against César. Miscalculating the feelings of Cornélie, Pompée's widow, he reveals the plot to her and is promptly denounced. In the battle that ensues, Ptolomée dies, and Cléopatre is restored to her throne. Cornélie, in spite of César's protestations, vows to continue her quest for vengeance until César joins Ptolomée in death.

By Corneille's own admission, this play contains the most "pompous" lines he ever penned. On the other hand, the play is entirely devoid of any real sentiments. Love is more akin to *galanterie* than to passion, and several of the roles, including the rather large one of Cléopatre, have but a tenuous connection to the central action. In view of these considerations, the immense popularity of the play during the seventeenth century and the first decades of the eighteenth is difficult to explain. In part, it may have been due to its declamatory nature, to which the contemporaries were far more receptive than later audiences; the temporal allusions may also have contributed to its vogue. It is quite likely that, when Corneille castigated advisors of lowly souls who misled kings (1193–94), he had Richelieu in mind, and it is quite possible that the seventeenth-century audience not only recognized this but saw its application to the times during which Mazarin influenced a very young Louis XIV and his mother. However, these considerations do not explain the success of the play during the last three or four decades of the reign of Louis XIV, for by then the temporal allusions must have lost all their punch and the *galant* declamations could not have been overly appreciated by a public used to Racine's verisimilitude and psychological realism.

These reservations notwithstanding, the play is worthy of attention, for it brings to the fore—however unsatisfactorily it may be—

the previously mentioned political preoccupations of the author. To better see this, a quick glance at the major protagonists is necessary.

With Cornélie and Cléopatre, Corneille reintroduces the juxtaposition first used in *Médée* and *Le Cid,* that of a feminine heroine with a more masculine one. Again, as in those two earlier plays, the feminine role is the minor one, Cornélie's purpose seeming to be to point up Cléopatre's defeminization. Cornélie, in love with Pompée, mourns his death and nurtures a hatred for his foes that is her new purpose in life: "I want to live with it and with it die" (1724). Cléopatre, on the contrary, as Corneille put it in his *Examen,* "is in love through ambition, . . . loving only where it can serve her aggrandisement." As a result, Pompée and César are equally loved by her because "one or the other will give me back my crown" (334). Thus prostituting herself out of a sense of duty— recalling Chimène's analogous reaction in similar circumstances— Cléopatre is sadly lacking in true femininity. Her ambition readily dismisses love, morality, even happiness (429–32), because a person such as she owes it to her birth to "make everything subservient to glory" (373). This explains her contempt for her brother who cannot define his duty without the help of Photin (644). As far as she is concerned, rulers can only find a viable path by searching their own souls.

Cornélie, though far more feminine, is no less generous. With the death of Pompée, her love has been transformed into an implacable hatred for his assassins and the man responsible for his death: César. Rejecting suicide or submission to the obvious generosity of César, she dedicates herself to her vengeance. If she saves César from the conspirators, it is because he must die through her, not in a political back-stage drama fomented by some Machiavellian mediocrities. Nor should the basic struggle within the breast of Cornélie be construed as one between love and duty, but rather between duty and generosity. Her love-turned-hate dictates that she seek the death of the man whose generosity commands her esteem. Saving César, she not only serves her duty by keeping her victim but also serves her generosity, since to allow a treasonable act is to take part in it (1385). As she puts it herself, her esteem and hatred are equal (1726), and both are equally justified: whereas her dutiful hatred may be considered existential there can be doubt that it is derived from her generous essence.

Although there can be little doubt as to César's generosity and sense of history, he does not reject whatever benefits he may derive from the actions of men such as Ptolomée. Calculating, he readily masters his love for the sage of his glory, but this mastery seems more the result of political deliberation that of a generous drive, and his tirades betray more the *galant* than the hero. As a result it is difficult to see him as anything more than a dramatic necessity, a pivot situated halfway between generosity and politics.

Youthful king surrounded by cunning and cynical advisors, Ptolomée succumbs to their advice and, to use a Cornelian term, degenerates to the point where he no longer understands either the situation or the people who control it. He is thus the clearest incarnation to date of self-defeating Machiavellianism: to be a good politician is to understand the people that are to be manipulated, but neither Ptolomée nor his advisers can grasp the nature of the love of César and Cléopatre. They completely misjudge César as a ruler; and when they decide to kill him, they confide in Cornélie, obviously visiting upon her their way of thinking, not realizing that, while she hates César, she admires him enough to save him from such mediocrities. At best, Ptolomée is what André Stegmann refers to as "false généreux." [26] His sense of justice is anything but generous (603), nor is his sense of duty to which he sacrifices everything, including his glory. Only in death might he be considered as regaining the merit that his station decrees.

Until *Pompée*, Corneille had presented heroes confronting outside forces: fate, destiny, the gods. While the gods are not totally absent—Ptolomée bemoans his "unfair" fate and sees fortune as his adversary (15–16, 41), Achillas agrees (118), but Cornélie trusts in the fairness of the gods (1737–40)—the play revolves around a totally different sort of struggle, one between two ideologies. Pompée never appears, César is a bad hero, Ptolomée is worse, Cornélie has a relatively minor role, and Cléopatre, for reasons already alluded to, is anything but attractive. The play, in short, has no hero because, unlike its predecessors, it does not put a human being but entire systems on trial. Corneille was very careful not to allow superior personalities to detract from fundamental verities.

The unity of the play resides in that theoretical struggle during which pompous tirades expounding generosity alternate with the most sinister postulation of political cynicism. In this struggle the Machiavellians often make use of a *généreux* dialectic, but without convincing or understanding the true *généreux*. This is simply because the two realms have little in common. "Justice is not a virtue of State," says one of Ptolomée's advisers (104). To spare Pompée is to recognize his virtues, but only by being blind to political facts. If there is disagreement among the advisers in the opening scene, it is not as to motives but as to the need to execute the defeated hero. Reasons of State (Corneille's capitals) dictate that Pompée be killed and Cléopatre be removed from the throne. Thus Photin guides Ptolomée into a path from which only an ultimate spark of generosity, his suicide, will save him. Thus viewed, *Pompée* can be seen as continuing the debate, begun in *Médée* and again made manifest in *Polyeucte*, between *médiocres* and *généreux*, or better still, between self-interest and moral rectitude. It is with this unequivocal condemnation of Machiavellianism that Corneille ended the cycle of political plays which only *L'Illusion comique* and his collaboration with the "Five" had interrupted.

CHAPTER 4

The Age of Melodrama

I *Le Menteur*

HAVING dismissed forever—he thought—the titanic struggles between Machiavellian and *généreux*, Corneille allowed himself to look back on these political plays in which a purely chivalrous love predominated, and smiled, a smile translated for posterity in a delightful self-parody.

Dorante, a provincial law student, has just landed in Paris. In the Tuileries Gardens, he sees Clarice with her cousin Lucrèce. Falling in love with Clarice, he thinks her name is Lucrèce because his servant tells him that such is the name of the most beautiful one. Dazzled by the company and the magnificent surroundings, he boasts of imaginary military exploits in order to dazzle in turn. His lies provoke the jealousy of Alcippe, Clarice's lover. Géronte, Dorante's father, wants his son to marry Clarice, but Dorante, because of the error in names, thinks that it is Lucrèce that is being forced on him. To evade the problem he tells his father that he is already married, and when Géronte wants to meet his new daughter-in-law, Dorante tells him that she is pregnant and cannot travel. When all the lies are finally revealed, Dorante is forced to give up Clarice to Alcippe and to marry Lucrèce, a solution that is far from distressing, as he announces that he loves her already.

The parodic effects can be seen at many levels. First, there is the obvious broad parody of heroic characters in the person of Dorante, dazzled as were the heroes of the great tragedies, but lacking the essential generosity of these. It also exists at a more specific level, with constant references to plays such as *Le Cid.* Thus the famous challenge of Rodrigue by his father is echoed by the ludicrous third scene of the last act in which Géronte catches his son in *flagrante delicto,* as it were; and Rodrigue's proud narration of the battle against the Moors, ending with "and the battle

ceased for lack of foes" is closely paralleled by the description
of a fictitious feat whose pleasures are halted by the light of day
(I, 5). It should further be added that the title is deceiving. We
are not dealing here with a liar, but with many liars, all intent on
proving that fraud in love is legitimate in spite of the lesson that
Rodrigue had been obliged to give to his father (1063–64).

Only one character, Dorante, really stands out, though a few
words about some of the others are appropriate. Whereas some
of the older characters of the tragedies were odious by their
obtuseness, Géronte only manages to be ridiculous. Good natured,
intent solely on his son's happiness, he constantly puts him in em-
barrassing positions without ever realizing the extent of the trouble he creates. Obviously lacking his son's nimble brains, he never
realizes that he comes very close to being the buffoon in the eyes
of the characters as well as those of the spectators. The girls,
particularly Clarice, are witty, able and willing to lie as well as
Dorante, and forever willing to flirt, without any regard for the
true meaning of love. Clarice consistently forgets that she is betrothed, and both girls are more interested in a man than in love.

Dorante stands out, but as curiously monofaceted: all the public really knows of him is that he loves to lie, enjoying the thought
of besting others' stories with his own (362–68). This has often
been considered a weakness of the play, yet it need not be one: if
Dorante were "alive," the viewer would worry about his moral
character, his "degeneration." [1] From such a viewpoint the play
would disintegrate: why should we worry about an ending that
makes no difference to the principals? What could possibly be
learned from a play that ends with the admonition to "learn how
to lie"? As it is, Dorante fails to appeal, so do the other characters,
and what might otherwise be a weakness in a serious play simply
becomes the easy ending of a light piece of entertainment dealing with quite unsubstantial characters. That is the real joy of the
parody: without heroic essence Dorante's quest is never more
than a game that not even he can take seriously, namely, the confrontation with his father. Rodrigue not only wished to be something but had to struggle to achieve his aim. Dorante has only to
lie to become his own heroic creation. He incarnates the "heroic
lie" at its lowest possible denominator, a game of wit. It is this
concept of life that leads to the original mixup: relying on wit,
he sees beauty as closely tied to it; since Clarice is the wittier of

the girls, she is also the more beautiful. To a servant relying on purely physical criteria, Lucrèce is the better looking of the two. When Dorante tires of the game—probably because it has gone out of hand and he is now its victim—Clarice's supremacy evaporates.

There are other aspects of *Le Menteur* that recall previous efforts: the constant confusion of appearances and reality (405 et seq.); the miraculous transformations, be they of one person into another—student into soldier, bachelor into husband, Clarice into Lucrèce—or of entire countrysides and cities; the mingling of tones; the sparkling style and rapid dialogue that allow four speeches in a single line, such as the opening of the fifth scene:

> Last night?
> > Last night.
> > > Beautiful?
> > > > Marvelous. (230)

This *élan vital*, reminiscent of *L'Illusion comique,* was never again to appear in the work of Corneille.

But if *Le Menteur,* like *L'Illusion,* can be considered a résumé of the past, it is also the harbinger of the future. The hints of melodrama, the crowded plot in which difficulties seem to pile on with little justification other than the author's desire to demonstrate his virtuosity, that is the stuff of which are made the plays of Corneille from *Le Menteur* to *Pertharite.*

II *La Suite du Menteur*

There can be no better example of this new trend than *La Suite du Menteur,* a melodramatic cloak-and-dagger play with merely the most tenuous of connections to its predecessor. Motivated undoubtedly by the success of *Le Menteur* (to which there are several references within *La Suite*), Corneille wrote a sequel, keeping Dorante and his servant Cotin, yet radically changing everything else that might have appealed to the original public.

Dorante, afraid of marriage, has absconded with Lucrèce's dowry. Having witnessed a duel in which a man is killed, he is arrested as the culprit and jailed, refusing to betray Cléandre, the real guilty party. Mélisse, the latter's sister, moved by Dorante's generosity—a word absent in *Le Menteur,* used frequently in *La Suite*—falls in love with him and he with her. A friend,

Philiste, causes Dorante's release and he is on the verge of marrying Mélisse when he finds out that Philiste loves her. Out of gratitude he steps aside, but Philiste, equally noble, refuses the sacrifice.

As can be surmised from the above, Dorante is a radically changed man. One may wonder how such a "generous" and noble man could abscond with a dowry and leave his fiancée in the lurch, but that is part of the play's prehistory. During the play he is above reproach. True, on several occasions he lies, but each lie is justified by the noble intent of saving someone even at the cost of self-sacrifice. In the dedicatory letter, Corneille admitted that Dorante had lost all his charm, but that is not his main failing which resides in the fact that he is never sure of the path he is to follow, hesitating in his noble designs and uneasy in his decisions.

The play is further hampered by an unfortunate admixture of tones. Although still funny, *La Suite* often verges on the bathetic. There is constant confusion, not only in the minds of characters such as Dorante (1059–63) or his valet Cliton (357), but also of the reader. Some of the reader's uneasiness may be traced to the metamorphosed Dorante; most of it is due to Cliton, a major role in this play. Possibly to suit the actor who created the role (Jodelet), possibly to enhance what little true comedy there is, Cliton sticks his nose into everything and enters into every conversation, with or without valid reasons. In the dedicatory letter, Corneille conceded that there was a big difference between the wit of a gentleman such as Dorante and the buffoonery of a servant. This is particularly true of a valet who seems to delight in debasing things beyond his comprehension and people better than he. Throughout the play there is the intertwining of two couples, each one on its own level: Dorante-Mélisse and Cliton-Lyse. Such a situation could have been palatable had the servants merely acted as a light counterpoint to offer comic relief. Unfortunately, Cliton is allowed to stupidly mock ideals he cannot grasp. As a result, he soon grates on the nerves, his cheap and ill-timed sarcasms merely showing the estrangement that keeps him from realizing that the Dorante of *La Suite* is not the Dorante of *Le Menteur*.

In view of this, it should not surprise us that the play as a whole was a dismal failure. Some years later, around 1650, it had a mild revival of favor whose reasons have remained a mystery to this day. If *La Suite du Menteur* deserves any attention today, it is, as has been stated above, as harbinger of things to come. In that sense, this last comedy of Corneille [2] continues the trend of *Le Menteur*. Of perhaps even greater interest is the treatment of love, and the contemporaries were quick to seize the novelty, memorizing and discussing lines from a play they otherwise held in rather low esteem. In *Médée*, Créuse had rejected a man (Ægée) although she claimed to admire him more than the man she loved. Her sincerity may well be questioned, but that is not the point. What is so is that even this dubious case is the lone exception to a rule observed in all the plays discussed in the previous chapter whereby esteem commands love. In this play— as in so many that will follow—the heroine falls in love not because of esteem, but because of "Heaven's orders" (1221). In lines that were on every contemporary's tongue (1221–34) and which come close to being a parody of Pascal's "the heart has its reasons, which reason does not know," she proclaims the sureness of her heart's drive for its predestined mate. Whatever admiration she may have for Dorante comes much later, when his actions command it. In the meanwhile, she had "sensed" his merit and loves without reservations, without comprehension. The public of the 1640's rightfully rejected the play, but with equal acumen and foresight retained those lessons from it.

III   *Rodogune*

Corneille was never again to write a true comedy, but *Le Menteur* and *La Suite* cannot, for all that, be considered as a hiatus. As I have stated already, certain elements, absent in plays such as *Le Cid* and *Cinna*, were obvious in these two comedies, and they reappear in *Rodogune*, suggesting that Corneille did not necessarily associate them with a specific type of play but had adopted them as new norms in his dramaturgy. *Rodogune*, Corneille's favorite, has been treated very severely by modern critics, perhaps because it is anything but "Cornelian," an adjective derived from the appreciation of the great tetralogy. It is a strange sort of deductive reasoning that allows general rules to be formulated from the reading of a few plays—all from a very short span of years—and that forces these standards willy-nilly on subsequent plays. One need not share Corneille's preference to see in

Rodogune a play as rigorouly constructed as any, though predicated on a somewhat different set of values.

This does not mean that everything about *Rodogune* is new and different. The notion of generosity is still omnipresent as is the idea (central to Corneille throughout his life) that overriding any concepts dealing with psychological realism, the characters have to be extraordinary to be dramatically viable. The situations of this play, reduced to their absolute essentials, are almost banal: young men torn between love and filial duty, conflicts between generosity and amorality, values and expediency. But under the pen of Corneille, these dramatic commonplaces are presented in extreme cases that simultaneously defy the laws of verisimilitude yet command attention and involvement, either through admiration or one of the more standard feelings such as fear, pity, or horror.

In spite of a very complicated plot the play is remarkably well constructed. The entire first act is a very involved exposition during which we learn that Cléopatre, queen of Syria, has twin sons, Antiochus and Séleucus; that the older will obtain the throne and Rodogune; that both sons love Rodogune more than the throne, but that only one is loved in return; and that Rodogune fears Cléopatre, who has hated her since her now dead husband nearly set her aside to marry Rodogune. Acting in jealousy and hatred as much as to preserve her position, Cléopatre had killed her husband and, in fact, has no intention of yielding up her present power to Rodogune through one of her sons. As of the second act the extent of Cléopatre's feelings are revealed: she has kept secret the order of birth of her two sons, for as long as it remains secret neither can reign and she can control both. She summons them to offer the throne to whichever kills Rodogune. The sons refuse, and Rodogune retaliates by offering to marry whichever son kills his mother.

At this stage the two brothers stop acting like twins: Séleucus, truly generous, rebels and withdraws, while Antiochus tries to adapt, urged by the news that it is he who is loved by Rodogune. When the mother attempts to set one brother against the other, only Séleucus really sees through her, though both refuse Cléopatre's propositions, their love for each other winning out over the ambition to which she was making appeal. Cléopatre then decides to kill all three of her opponents. She stabs Séleucus and

pours poison into a nuptial cup destined for Antiochus and Rodogune, but the news of the death of his brother reaches Antiochus
before he can drink. The last words of Séleucus, as reported, are
sufficiently ambiguous to cast suspicion on both women. To clear
herself and urge Antiochus to drink the poison, Cléopatre drinks
some herself, but the poison acts so rapidly that she dies, cursing
Antiochus and Rodogune, before they can drink.

Corneille was justifiably proud of the inventiveness demonstrated in this play, but the structure is no less admirable. Each
act has one major scene, each such scene is carefully prepared
and followed by a detailed exposition of the effects of the crisis on
the participants. Only the last act is a straightforward action, a
numbing crescendo of the highest dramatic caliber. It is, of course,
melodrama, but at what a level! Furthermore, each of the first
four acts ends in suspense. At the end of the first act several
questions are left unanswered: Who is the older son? Who will
marry Rodogune? Is Cléopatre sincere? Which of the brothers is
loved by Rodogune? Not all these questions are answered in the
second act, which ends with an additional riddle, Séleucus having
announced a plan to solve all the problems. In the third act that
plan is revealed: Rodogune is to declare her choice and the
elected will have both crown and princess; but Rodogune, with
her impossible ultimatum, leaves us wondering as to the outcome.
In Act IV we learn of Cléopatre's decision to seek a total vengeance, again leaving us to contemplate the possible results of such
a resolution. All of these suspensions are finally distilled in the
climactic moment when Antiochus puts the fatal cup to his lips.
And throughout, as P. J. Yarrow has pointed out, Corneille "skill-
fully alternates moments of tension with moments of tranquility
within each act." [3]

Yarrow is quite right of course, but Octave Nadal is no less so
when he deplores that rigorous structure and, in so doing, points
to one of the basic flaws of the play: everything in *Rodogune* is
subjugated to the structure, and for the sake of dramatic effect
psychological truth has at times been stretched,[4] though ironically,
less in the monstrous mother than in the other characters.

It is impossible to study the characters of this play without
wondering why it was called *Rodogune* and not *Cléopatre*. It has
often been suggested that the latter would have made people
think of the heroine of *Pompée*, but it is nevertheless true that

Cléopatre is the dominating character of this play from beginning to end. If I treat them here side by side it is not for the sake of some unfair comparison but to better view their respective drives.

In several of the previously studied plays, and in almost all of those that follow, there are two heroines, one feminine, one masculine, testing their respective modes in similar crises. This juxtaposition is as obvious in *Rodogune* as it had been in *Médée, Le Cid,* or *Pompée.* Rodogune, although ready to follow the dictates of her duty (373–80, 930–38), has fallen in love for reasons she cannot comprehend (362). Like the Infante, she readily resolves this inner conflict. She seems feminine compared to Cléopatre, but still lacks the tenderness so obvious in the later plays. Cléopatre is entirely "unsexed." Her main motive is a lust for power (423). Her husband's infidelity concerned her only insofar as it threatened this thirst (464–66). This difference between the two women is nowhere made more manifest than in the motives behind the proposition presented to the two brothers: Cléopatre merely wants to rid herself of any rival; Rodogune wishes to forestall disaster. As Corneille has suggested in the *Examen,* Rodogune knows that neither brother will accept her challenge and thus force her to choose. The last lines of her request make its insincerity quite manifest. To make the proposition seem sincere an actress would have to make Rodogune as harsh and cruel as Cléopatre, and the lines just do not permit that. Moreover, Rodogune cannot compete dramatically with Cléopatre on the latter's terms and with the latter's weapons.

Cléopatre is a monomaniac whose obsession for power, rigorously and logically presented, demands a total sacrifice that even includes herself. Amoral, if not immoral, she is as incapable of communications with the *généreux* as her predecessors had been. If one looks at the usual struggle between passion and duty or natural behavior, she is totally given over to passion, oblivious to the call of nature. Hatred, jealousy, lust for power are her motives for her husband's death, her campaign against Rodogune and her own sons. Devious, without the least scruples, she is far more monstrous than Médée who had at least some justification for her acts, since, as I stated earlier, these could be interpreted as attempts at redemption, both for her and her children. Médée was inhuman in the name of human dignity. Cléopatre's "leave my heart, nature" (1491) ends the fourth act; the first lines of the fifth show her gloating over the death of one of her sons (1497) and rejecting any tender or virtuous feelings she might have for the survivor whom she disowns (1510–14) and eventually curses.

Rodogune has feelings too, but *généreuse,* she is too aware of her obligations to rank and origin to allow these feelings to reign. The closer she is to the crown, the greater her servitude: "We have no heart to love or hate/ All our passions know but to obey" (869–70). To Cléopatre, the throne means power; to Rodogune, obligations. It is this duality that makes the duplicity of Cléopatre all the more successful in that, just as Machiavellians always judge the others by their own standards, so do the *généreux,*[5] and her sons will, for some time, think only well of Cléopatre. By the same token, the fact that Rodogune sees through her first, yet refuses to believe her, may well indicate that she is not quite as generous as the two men.

The juxtaposition is then easy to see, but there is another one, parallel to the first, within the heart of one of the protagonists. More and more the maturing Corneille will show the heroic lie, that oppressive mask, having problems with a heart that "murmurs, and tames itself regretfully" (*Œdipe,* 796), one that can be subdued only after a long and painful struggle.

Rodogune is the first of these heroines that are so split. Ready to follow the path dictated by duty, this princess succumbs to love. Torn between these two feelings, she opts for self-sacrifice. There is nothing new in this: the Infante had done no less. There is a new aspect to the sacrifice, however: the Infante had given that which she *could* not take herself. To save her honor she rejected an impossible marriage. Rodogune, to do justice to her sense of self, consciously besmirches her personal glory with a gesture that is necessary, yet base. As I stated earlier, her request is made to prevent strife between the brothers; more important still, it is a freely chosen gesture which must be considered as the beginning of a transformation in Corneille's concept of the perfect tragic heroine. All tragic heroes are alone, but while in the earlier plays their solitude is forced on them by contingencies, with Rodogune we see the first hint of a trend that will blossom a few plays later, one dealing with the very nature of Cornelian tragedy: the inner solitude, self-imposed, goes far beyond the usual peril of life found in the earlier plays. It is precisely this solitude that is consecrated by Rodogune's sacrificial proposition—and no less by Séleucus' retirement.

This brings up the question of the twin brothers. They are remarkably alike in some ways, yet with delicate nuances separating them, Séleucus being the more sensitive, the more lucid of the two. One of the flaws of *Rodogune* is that in this play, where evil is the driving force, the *généreux* are relatively undramatic. Antiochus forever trusts that virtue will triumph, and both brothers do little more than submit—with laudable steadfastness—to events that are quite beyond their control. Unlike Horace, Rodrigue, Auguste, or even Médée, the *généreux* are here anything but heroic. This is due to a fundamental aspect of tragedy heretofore neglected by Corneille whereby man is called upon to seek a truth which, when perceived and understood, will make all future action impossible. As Nietzsche said in *The Birth of Tragedy*, "Insight kills action, the veiled through illusion is necessary for action." [6] The two brothers are alike in that, when their mother reveals herself in all her savage fury, they are stripped of their power to act. To the extent that Antiochus can keep a few illusions (his hope that nature and goodness might yet prevail), he continues to struggle. Séleucus, more lucid, simply retires from the struggle, surrendering both his political and his amorous ambitions.

In previous plays, each danger allowed the hero to further demonstrate his courage, his valor, his generosity. Here this is also true, but there comes a moment when Séleucus can no longer play the game, and he withdraws. As Robert Nelson has so aptly seen, Séleucus (foreshadowing the last hero of Corneille, Suréna) "rejects ambition in this world in terms which cast doubt on the very ideal of worldly ambition"; unlike Polyeucte, he does not even trade in this ideal for a transcending one. [7] His final "Adieu" to his mother, following his assertion that he lacks neither eyes nor heart (1472–75), is one of the most deeply touching passages of this or any other play, comparable in many ways to the farewell of Bérénice in Racine's play by that name.

To be sure, not everything about *Rodogune* is innovative. A single horrible character dominating the stage and romanesque aspects of the play are certainly reminiscent of *Médée*. The instinctive love of Rodogune for Antiochus is very much like that of

Chimène for Rodrigue. In both cases two suitors seem to be of equal merit, yet only one is loved. Events soon prove the superiority of the preferred lover. This clairvoyant love was particularly important in *La Suite du Menteur*, where the man was an unknown quantity to the woman mysteriously smitten. Here, in a tragedy, such fantasy could not have been permitted, and Rodogune merely senses in two noble souls the one that will remain closer to his sense of self.

The optimistic ending is also a carry over from the previous plays. From the beginning Antiochus trusts in divine justice, and with each assault on his optimism he calls out to the gods. On the verge of drinking the poison he does so again, and the gods obviously intervene, allowing a legitimately happy ending for the play. Superimposed on a "human nature that is perverted or virtuously powerless, [there is] the presence of an unfailing, transcending Justice" [8] as there had been in so many of the previous tragedies.

On the other hand, many of the aspects of earlier plays present in *Rodogune* show subtle yet important changes. Some have already been discussed; a few remain to be. As in *La Suite*, "There are secret ties, there are sympathies" (359) that seek to rule Rodogune, and, though duty is stronger (378), love and esteem are no longer synonymous. In the previous plays, pride and glory had been concepts closely allied to some moral notions. Even Horace, fanatic though he may be, is reluctant to kill his sister and can hardly be considered as reveling in the thought or the act. Not so with Cléopatre: no more scruples hinder her, and the opening lines of the last act show her gloating over the fact that the death of Séleucus has rid her of an enemy. Nor is she the only character affected by this disease. Rodogune has a strange code of ethics, and Antiochus is not overly demanding. Only Séleucus seems entirely moral, and his fate is far from enviable. This radical departure from the ideal world of Rodrigue and Auguste is perhaps the major innovation of *Rodogune*. Blending melodramatic moments more worthy of *précieux* novels than of the author of *Cinna* with the energetic, concise, almost brutal language for which he was justly famous, Corneille had not only managed to recreate the tension so typical of his earlier works but had in the process found a novel dramaturgy.

IV   *Théodore*

After *Rodogune* came *Théodore,* or rather, after Cléopatre, Marcelle—two women, each one given over to a single idea, willing to sacrifice everything to it, using every device and tool imaginable to realize their goal. The play, whose full title is *Théodore, vierge et martyre,* was called "Christian tragedy" by its author, a label which, as shall be seen, is far from accurate.

Placide, son of the governor of Antioch, loves Théodore and refuses to marry Flavie his stepsister, whose mother Marcelle then decides to have Théodore killed to get her out of the way. Upon learning that Théodore is Christian, Marcelle decides instead to force her into a house of prostitution from which Didyme, a young Christian, helps her to escape. Caught, Didyme is condemned to death. Théodore tries to save him and is also condemned. Shortly after Théodore's escape, Flavie succumbs to a fit of rage, and Marcelle, remorseful, kills herself.

Although Corneille called *Théodore* "Christian," as he had *Poleyucte,* it is not for all that a Christian play. Its main action deals with conflicts originating in erotic and political rivalries, and the religion of the martyrs is far more Cornelian than Christian. Furthermore, the major protagonists are Placide and Marcelle with Théodore as passive as the two brothers of *Rodogune.* Her passivity, moreover, is easy to explain: faced with an impossible choice between idolatry and unchastity, she rejects a choice which is cowardly and shameful in itself (769–74). In that moment of total insight, of decision, she is as fully tragic as Séleucus, but, equally undramatic, she is no match for either Placide or his stepmother.

The play was a failure. After five performances it never saw the stage again in Paris, though it enjoyed a modest success in the provinces. The reasons for this failure are numerous. There is, first of all, the ever-present question of decency: the public of the 1640's must have been shocked by the thought of a saintly virgin among the prostitutes. But even more fundamental is the problem of dramatic coherence. To better see this it is necessary to first cast a glance on some of the main characters. Valens, the governor of Antioch, is one of those mediocrities so successfully presented by Corneille. *"Faux généreux,"* he tries to act noble but settles for clever politics and safety afforded by such a path (1756–66).

And yet, as André Stegmann has noted, in all his pettiness, Valens is more touching than the truly generous Placide,[9] who commands our admiration but little else. Marcelle is by far the strongest character in the play, a mean virago with thought only for the happiness of a daughter who is dying off-stage, and utter contempt for her cowed husband. To her belong what are undoubtedly the best lines of the play, but that is not the problem, which lies with the titular heroine. Moved by a pure love of God that gives rise to her wish of chastity—but a strange type of chastity, devoid of any sense of humility, a proud virtue predicated on will, whereby, if will is not voluntarily involved, then the downfall is immaterial—she rejects both Didyme and Placide, one Christian, one pagan. This is why Marcelle condemns her to shame rather than death, in the hope that Placide would then reject her. But this danger, however logical it may be, is at the root of the dramatist's problem. Dramatically, what interests the reader or viewer is Théodore's reaction to her danger. But how can a virgin verbalize it? Corneille had to substitute long and frequently tedious tirades and recitations.

Compounding this flaw is one in the plot itself. Once Théodore is saved from the house of shame the play should be over. But she returns, assured that her honor and virtue are safe. Marcelle, who now must avenge her daughter's death, decides on a lesser punishment, death, and kills Didyme and Théodore with her own hands. In the last act the characters seem as intransigent and impervious as those of a bad comedy. As a result, the play has no resolution, no *dénouement*, just an ending.

This is not to say that the play is a total loss. The scenes of confrontation in which Marcelle stands up to all by her implacable hatred, her powerful passion for her daughter, a sickly girl we never see on stage, continue the trend begun in *Rodogune* and seem, in an anachronistic way perhaps, like a testing ground for the great villainesses of the plays to come. The verbal duels with the youthful and exuberant Placide are quite successful, and the confrontation between Marcelle and Théodore (II, 4) is as dramatic as any scene in Corneille. In this truly great scene, "two women who hate each other are outwardly polite, their antagonism expressing itself through irony, until the mask falls and the hostility becomes overt."[10] It is this fine nursing along of a crescendo that marks the entire construction of *Rodogune,* and it will be a trademark of the "middle" Corneille.

Should one see in *Théodore* a hiatus, a beginning, or an end? Or rather what Corneille saw in it in 1660, when he wrote his *Examen,* namely that he had made a mistake, chosen a bad topic and treated it not too well, hesitating between several modes and doing justice to none.

Just as there was no one to really offset Cléopatre, there is no one here to balance Marcelle, and Placide, in all his generosity and heroism, is no dramatic match for his monstrous stepmother. This is not to say that the two women are alike: Cléopatre was motivated by purely selfish drives; the political ambitions of Marcelle are all at the service of her maternal drive, a desperate devotion to a dying daughter. As André Stegmann points out, Corneille could have made her truly tragic; instead, he made her needlessly odious at the end (1817–20). As a result, instead of two contradictory but equally valid principles, we have one side undramatic but virtuous, another dramatically attractive but morally repulsive. There is little doubt that for once Corneille's moral optimism led him astray.[11]

Théodore supposedly deals with a strangely inactive heroine of will. More troubling still is the fact that it deals with a love of God subjugated to political machinations or, worse still, religion adopted and adapted by politicians. As Octave Nadal states, *Théodore* suffers from Corneille's reluctance to center the play on a Christian ethos exclusively. Théodore is an unyielding Cornelian heroine, not just a Christian in love with Christ, a *généreuse* for whom chastity is her glory, and whose guilt is determined by her will, or rather whose refusal to contribute to her guilt absolves her.[12] Corneille was not to repeat that mistake; he never again wrote a "Christian tragedy."

V *Héraclius*

With the success of *Rodogune* and the failure of *Théodore* in mind, Corneille once again turned to a bare subject suggested by history to which he could add all the Romanesque and melodramatic details that his inventive mind could supply. The major knot of the plot, a child substitution, was at the time a novelistic commonplace, and not unknown in the realm of tragicomedy. This raised a fundamental question of taste. After all, had not the

French recently decided that tragedy and tragicomedy were not of the same fiber and that the former should be predicated on simple and elevated events whose verisimilitude is above question? Corneille knew that he was being daringly different and defended his approach in an *Avis au lecteur,* in which he redefined verisimilitude as concerning only the matter within the play, not *"extra fabulam,"* such as the actual child substitution, and dealing only with the psychology and development of the characters and the action, not with the dramatic a priori.[13] This audacious note is of extreme importance, but it should not be considered as a landmark in itself, for Corneille had already, by his past production, shown his predilection for the extraordinary. That was the real nature of Cornelian innovation, and of Cornelian melodrama: whereas, in the days of the tetralogy, we had been witnesses to dialectical debates about possible paths to heroism, we are now held in suspense by the numerous ups and downs of the protagonists' fortunes. As Antoine Adam put it, Corneille became entrapped by the pleasure of creating powerful intrigues with extraordinarily energetic heroes, unaware that posterity would prefer the moral dilemma of an Auguste or the passion of a Pauline.[14]

The plot of *Héraclius* is one of the most complicated that Corneille devised, far more complex than *Rodogune's.* Corneille admitted (or boasted?) that it had to be seen more than once to be understood. Even reduced to its bare essentials it makes for complicated reading: Phocas, an usurper, has massacred the entire family of Maurice, the emperor of Constantinople, allowing only Pulchérie to survive, or so he thinks, because Pulchérie's youngest brother Héraclius has been secretly spared and raised at court as Martian son of Phocas, while the real Martian has been raised as the governess' dead son Léonce. To cement his position, Phocas wants to unite his "son" to Pulchérie who, however, loves the real Martian, that is, Léonce. With the peril of incest imminent, the governess reveals her fraud, presents the two men, and challenges Phocas: "Guess if you can, and choose, if you dare" (1408). This climactic scene is shortly followed by the assassination of Phocas and the proposed union of the young people, Héraclius marrying Eudoxe (daughter of the governess), Martianus marrying Pulchérie, and the two families being united by an oath of eternal friendship between the two young men, a union which had been projected on a Machiavellian level by Phocas.

As may be surmised, the characters of *Héraclius* are not nearly as interesting as is the interplay. Still, a few words are in order. In spite of the title the central character is the tyrant Phocas. Evil, lucid, cynical, without scruples, he is a worthy descendant of Cléopatre and Marcelle. Corneille, however, had learned a lesson, and he took great pains not to have this giant box with mere shadows. Martian and Héraclius are worthy opponents, and the scene of renunciation (IV, 3) in which both young men prefer death to recognition as the tyrant's son is far more successful than the corresponding scene in *Rodogune*. Despite this, the best that can be said for the youthful pair is that their generosity is measured by their stand and stance against Phocas, whose real antagonist is Léontine, the governess. She has a single goal, and nothing can distract her. She is not only happy with the pain she inflicts on Phocas, but oblivious to the difficulties she imposes as well on those she supposedly loves. She is as implacable an avenger as any Corneille ever created, and makes us view the younger characters as little more than her tools. As such, their feelings and self-doubt concern her little if at all; once the spectator grasps this, the focus switches to the truly tragic Phocas-Léontine struggle. Pulchérie does not detract from that either. Her hatred is stronger than any love she might have, and while it gives rise to some of her best lines, it shows her as too rigid to hold our interest. Her dilemma is not unlike that of Chimène, and she even takes on some of the latter's lines: Chimène had been willing to give herself to any knight avenging her (1401-2); Pulchérie, in her excesses lacking the sense of decorum of Chimène, is willing to give herself to the vilest slave were he to kill Phocas (1047-50).

Overriding all other considerations in this play is the omnipresence of doubt, which makes the characters unsure of themselves and of each other, and is finally used as a weapon by both Héraclius and Léontine. Against this mood, all the conventional weapons —the "call of blood," generosity, and so forth—are without effect. This doubt, however, at no time shakes the protagonists' notion of right and wrong. Values are never in doubt, particularly for Martian and Héraclius, and it is this consideration more than any other that keeps the play from lapsing into the comic. Pulchérie's sense of values is unwavering too. When forced to change erotic into fraternal love, she simply states that as honor aroused her passion, duty will calm it (838). Her desire for vengeance makes her refuse to marry the son of Phocas, since such a marriage would bring about a conflict between her duty to avenge her former family and her duty to her new one. This sense of duty, which even outweighs her desire for glory, makes her sacrifice her love to her hatred.

What *Héraclius* really puts in doubt is the heretofore unassailable notion of generosity. The last act—from the opening *stances* to the long debate of scene 2, to the very moment when the issue is settled—the normal criteria for discerning generosity are impotent. A moment before he learns his real identity, Héraclius still refers to himself as "whoever I may be" (1886). From this uncertainty is born one of the few touching moments of the play: as Rodogune had been willing to besmirch her glory, so is Héraclius in his willingness to accept the stigma of being the son of the tyrant.[15] The irony is that such a will to sacrifice does more harm to the Machiavellian tyrant than to the *généreux*.

One of the subtler ironies in the play is its handling of the Machiavellian themes. Presented here in perhaps their purest statement in Corneille, they are completely foiled. Machiavelli had stated that there are two methods in political endeavors, one human, one animal, and that where the former fails, it is proper to resort to the latter. In *Héraclius*, that is exactly what is said: "Violence is just where gentleness is ineffective" (89). But how can one fight one's foe with either if that foe is not known? Phocas is neutralized not because he cannot understand a generous world, but simply because he does not know the identity of his enemy. The irony of the stalemate is enhanced with our knowledge that it is predicated on a flaw in this would-be Machiavellian: Cléopatre would have acted, ridding herself of both Martian and Héraclius; but Phocas needs a son to perpetuate his name. His escape from Horace's dreaded "eternal becoming" can only be realized through a son. Thence his pitiful position in which he begs for a son when his dead rival, Maurice, has two.

In such a play there can be no *dénouement*, only an ending. No one is satisfied, not Pulchérie in her hatred, not the tyrant in his search for continuum, not Martian pursuing his identity, and certainly not Héraclius seeking to prove his friendship through self-sacrifice. What solution there is to the basic plot comes from

outside, from a factor barely hinted at before, a dissatisfied subject who kills the tyrant for reasons which, however legitimate
they may be, seem quite unrelated to the plot. This ending is a
deus ex machina type in more ways than one: at the elementary
level it is the author rescuing his play from an impasse; on another level, as line 1914 points out, it is God settling an issue
which could not be resolved by human means.[16]

Héraclius can be linked with many of the previous plays by the
themes of generosity, Machiavellian modes and failures, sacrifices, and others. But in the discussions centering on the specific
problems of usurpers there are heralds of a new concern of
Corneille, one to which he will return several times, particularly
during this period of his productivity which ends with *Pertharite,*
a play in which this particular problem is central. *Héraclius* is
not a perfect play—far from it—but it is an important one, one in
which Corneille reveals the road he was traveling during this
entire period, one in which we see the rigor with which he allowed the entire action to derive from a well-established a priori.
The ending is far from satisfactory, but the central action of the
play is no less logical for all that. Except for Léontine, all the
characters suffer from an impotence based on doubt, and in the
analysis of that feeling, in the search of these characters for
themselves, Corneille, without being untrue to his earlier tendencies, showed himself to be on his way—however haltingly—to
discover the rationale of his later masterpieces.

VI *Andromède*

In January 1650 a three-hour extravaganza was staged to the
delight of the Parisians avid of "machine-plays," productions in
which grandiose stage effects were part and parcel of the play,
if not its core and very reason for being. Corneille had been working on *Andromède* since 1647, but Vincent de Paul had talked the
queen-mother into opposing such lavish spectacles, and before
she could be mollified the Fronde had made its impact on the
theatrical activities of the capital. Mazarin, who had commissioned
the play, therefore had to wait nearly three years to see it but,
if contemporary accounts of the success are the least bit reliable,
was certainly not disappointed.

Andromède courted success in many ways. The music of Das-
soucy and the machines of Torelli were admired by all, and in his

Examen Corneille good-humoredly gave credit to these aspects of the performance that preempted his delightful versification. There were some very timely tirades on grace, for this was the age of Port-Royal and Jansenism. But when all is said and done, it is difficult not to agree with those critics who call it nothing more than a "charming parenthesis" in the production of Corneille, difficult to tie in with the plays of that period. If Corneille had been as greedy as some of his detractors claim, it might have been a very long parenthesis, for lyric opera was coming into its own, witness the success of Quinault and, to some extent, of Thomas Corneille. Much of this vogue was due to the solid backing the salon faithful gave to "tender tragedies." For the serious student of Corneille, it is fortunate that the author did not persist in mining this newly discovered vein. The play is interesting only in so far as it shows how radically Corneille could depart from his norms. How far his statements on love—"To expect reason to rule a lover is to be even more blind than he. A heart worthy of loving . . . surrenders entirely, examines nothing" (412–16)—are from Rodrigue's noble assertions or even the dithyrambic tirades of the lovers in the early comedies. There is no attempt to counterbalance the precious treatment of mythology and the supernatural by some kind of dramatic verisimilitude or unity. The ultimate apotheosis of the mortal protagonists can only reinforce a notion that any reader of *Andromède* must have from the first act on: that this romanesque and *précieux* extravaganza is a divertissement on a grand scale, but has little to do with Cornelian drama.

VII *Don Sanche d'Aragon*

Andromède was not the only play to suffer from the vicissitudes of the Fronde. *Don Sanche d'Aragon,* the next play, in which the contemporaries could find all the fashionable aspects of the *précieux* novels coupled with the proud declamations of a young knight that could not fail to remind them of Rodrigue, also contained some very timely allusions, and those were its undoing. At the outset, everyone applauded this "heroic comedy" whose basic situation—a queen without king trusting an adventurer with a somewhat obscure past—had much in common with the situation in France at that time. It is, therefore, not surprising, as Corneille tells us in his dedicatory letter, that *Don Sanche*'s success was only popular and that it failed to win the approval of an "illustrious voice." Though the provinces greeted it warmly, Paris discreetly decided that its original verdict must have been in error and relegated the play to a limbo which posterity decreed it deserved.[17]

A revolution having broken out in Aragon, the Queen and her daughter, Doña Elvire, have sought refuge at the court of Isabelle of Castille. At that court, Carlos, a young warrior of unknown origin, has made a reputation for himself and has fallen in love with the Queen, who also loves him, though she fights this passion for a man unworthy of her because of his base birth. She must instead select one of three "worthier" men, and asks Carlos to choose. He does so by challenging the three to duels, the one to defeat him being the future king; however, only Don Alvar, in love with Elvire, feels that he must accept. In the meanwhile, a search has begun for Don Sanche, the son of the dead king of Aragon, lost as a baby. It turns out that Carlos is Sanche. Worthy now of Isabelle, he reluctantly abandons the notion of a duel with Alvar and marries Isabelle, thus showing that his merits—obvious all along—were not derogations of the precepts of generosity, but its very proof.

As had been the case with most of the previous plays, *Don Sanche* again revealed Corneille's penchant for innovation, not the least of which is the play's label of "heroic comedy," which the author explains as being a play dealing with people worthy of tragedies, involved in matters of consequence described in elevated tones, but in which there is no real fear of death or disgrace as is the case in tragedy. In spite of this new label, *Don Sanche* has many links with the past. It shares its romanesque and melodramatic traits with all the plays of this period. More specifically, the danger of incest raised when Elvire, not yet knowing that Carlos is her long-lost brother, falls in love with him; the mystery surrounding the birth of the central character; an heir thought dead returning to claim his throne, his identity revealed or confirmed by an old note—all these ploys are familiar to readers of *Héraclius*.

Don Sanche owes an even greater debt to *Le Cid*. Isabelle, unable to wed a man worthy in every respect but station, recalls the Infante. Echoing Rodrigue's definition of knightly love, and his rejection of the role of *perfide amant*, Elvire asserts that "a heart belongs to no one when it belongs to two," for in this situation it is *"perfide"* to both (715–18). It is in this definition of love and its application that *Don Sanche* comes closest to *Le Cid*. Don Alvar, though in love with Doña Elvire, accepts the challenge of Carlos, not because he loves Isabelle but because his notion of glory will not let him do otherwise. He feels that, were he to reject the opportunity to win Isabelle, he would no longer be worthy of Elvire. This dilemma, like Rodrigue's, cannot be resolved without some deus ex machina—unavailable to Rodrigue—since beaten he is unworthy, and victorious, Isabelle's husband (764). Generosity is synonymous with *Le Cid*, and to a lesser extent with all the plays that followed. In *Don Sanche*, as one critic put it, "handsome does as handsome is." [18] Carlos may reject the merit of birth (247–50) and see his glory as existing in spite of his low birth (1641), but he only thinks he is self-made. The final identification of Carlos as Don Sanche shows that only kings act like kings; that only generosity, that is, birth, leads to truly glorious behavior. Every heretofore unexplainable attitude (the love of two royal ladies, the respect of a rival, the sympathy of the queen of Aragon, Carlos' valor itself) is explained by the revelation that Carlos is really Don Sanche. As Rodrigue had to prove that the trust put in him by two women—and an entire nation for that matter—was not misplaced, so must Carlos. Isabelle, by her love, selects a man whose real worth she cannot yet guess. The "secret" movements of her heart lead her to a man who must then prove that her choice was correct. With this reaffirmation of generosity *Don Sanche*, often considered a radical play, must be considered as one of Corneille's most politically orthodox.

Don Sanche is much more than a recapitulation of the past. Though the previous paragraphs suggest that it is a variation on some old themes, the variation has strong hints of the new themes that Corneille will shortly begin to exploit. It is in this interplay of the old and the new that *Don Sanche*, a play otherwise deserving of the limbo to which it has been relegated, is most interesting.

Certain aspects of Carlos' concept of love are not new, nor is the impasse in which it puts him (529–36): he loves Isabelle because of his esteem for her; were she to stoop so low as to return his love he would have to reassess his feelings, esteem her less, and love her less. But to this old concept is tied one not previously used by Corneille outside his comedies, namely, the physical side of love: immediately preceding his tirade on esteem Carlos has rapturously described the "celestial union" of charm and beauty in Isabelle (519–28).[19]

To put this in proper perspective, it must be said that Carlos first rhapsodizes about beauty, then catches himself and dissertates on his basic values. On the verge of becoming comic, Carlos returns to the heroic. This is not his monopoly. Seldom has Corneille put characters on stage more aware of their duty to themselves. Elvire knows what she is and what she owes to herself (68), and will not admit her love for Carlos. Isabelle readily states that she must be mistress of herself (120), but confesses her love, yet another incarnation of the ambivalent woman. On the other hand it is she who most readily uses a lover ready to submit to her every whim, unheeding of the cruelty of some of her requests, while Elvire, aloof though she may be, more readily understands Carlos' motives. The duality heretofore predominently manifest in the juxtaposition of two contrasting female personalities, has been given an inner echo which we will hear over and over again in the later plays of Corneille. In these later plays, the tragedy will not evolve out of a simple struggle between love and reasons of state, but out of the very nature of love. It is here that Isabelle is important in the understanding of the later heroines. When she hears that Don Sanche is alive, Isabelle immediately understands the implications of this new turn of events, not only in regard to her duty, but also in regard to her more personal feelings. It is clear that she cannot marry Carlos, but she does not want to see him and her archrival Elvire happy if she cannot be. She therefore decides to marry Don Sanche, thus becoming the queen of both Carlos and Elvire, and able to dictate a marriage for each, but not to each other. This is a complete reversal from the generous—in both senses of the word—attitude of *Le Cid's* Infante, and one which will be central in Corneille's last play, *Suréna*. In *Suréna*, it will spell death. Here, in a heroic comedy, it is nothing more than one of many melodramatic dreams that are never realized.

VIII *Nicomède*

In this long line of romanesque melodramas, *Nicomède* once again betrays Corneille's tendency to experiment, to innovate within the framework of his already tested ideas. In many of these adventurous experiments, Corneille failed to win the public's suffrage. Not this time. *Nicomède* was an immediate and lasting success, second only to *Le Cid* and *Cinna* during the seventeenth century.[20] The next two centuries did not share this enthusiasm, though the twentieth century has gone a long way toward a rehabilitation of the play and the original public's verdict. *Nicomède*, to use Corneille's own words in the *Examen*, is "rather extraordinary," and to bring his public something new the author had to deviate from the normal path. As a result, we have a very simple plot in which "tenderness and the passions, which must be the soul of tragedies, have no part."

Prusias, king of Bithynia, has a son from a previous marriage, Nicomède, and one from his present marriage to Arsinoë, Attale. Whereas Nicomède is proud and ready to defy the Roman conquerors of Bithynia, Attale is a docile vassal. Arsinoë, to further her son's chances at the throne, is constantly plotting to create new foes for Nicomède. Attale is also a rival of Nicomède for the hand of Laodice (queen of Armenia, who loves Nicomède) and in his attempts to win her is seconded by Flaminius, the Roman ambassador. When Arsinoë convinces her husband that Nicomède is plotting against him, Prusias, with the help of Flaminius, decides to get rid of this dangerous and bothersome son. Nicomède is about to be taken to Rome as hostage when Attale, recovering his generosity, saves him with the help of the sympathetic populace. Not to be outdone, Nicomède gives back to his father the throne which the people wanted him to have; his father, Félix to the end, then tries to reconcile all sides in order to safeguard his beleaguered position.

There is no doubt that, in spite of its simple plot, *Nicomède* retains many aspects of the novel and of melodrama. Although the basic plot is simple, the devious machinations of the politicians give rise to strange involvements, complicated intrigues with accusations and counteraccusations. The rapid changes of fortune: the reversal of form whereby Attale, like Alvar, shows his generous potential and contributes to the happy ending; the recognition scene, complete with a ring given by Nicomède to his masked savior whereby he recognizes that savior;[21] the flawless hero who leaves his victorious armies to fly to the aid of his ladylove; the ruthlessly amoral stepmother—all these are but a few of

the many elements of *Nicomède* straight out of the salon literature
of the times, and which link the play to those that immediately
preceded it.[22]

Nicomède is, however, much more than just another melodrama. It is the minute analysis of a psychology reminiscent of
the tetralogy. By its main themes *Nicomède* not only recalls these
great plays but shows that the author, his desire for novelty notwithstanding, has not changed his basic tenets. Corneille's theater
is ever predicated on the notion of generosity, yet one may well
wonder about the meaning of that word in a theater in which the
younger generation forever instructs the older, not only as to paths
of action, but concerning the fundamental nature of things. As
Rodrigue gave his father lessons in honorable love, Nicomède
now teaches his father the art of ruling. When Prusias complains
of the struggle within him between father and husband, Nicomèdes points out that neither has the right to him. In a mono-
syllabic reply worthy of Médée or the Old Horace, Nicomède
shows his father what life is all about. When Prusias hesitates between love and nature, between the roles of husband and father,
Nicomède has a simple answer.

> Be neither one nor the other.
>
> What must I be?
>
> King. (1318)

As had been the case of Médée, of Rodrigue, and of so many
others, such a position demands the sacrifice, not of self, but of a
baser interest of that self, the gratification of passions, for the
sake of a higher good. All of Médée's problems derived from a
momentary lapse. The only difference here is that Prusias' "degeneration" is not a momentary one.

As in the previous plays, Corneille presents the *généreux*
against the Machiavellians. From Corneille's prefatory statements,
one might assume that *Nicomède* is just another work about
Rome, and in a way it is, but not in the way of *Cinna* or *Horace*.
Nicomède is a hero totally engaged in defying Rome, an entity
unto himself, who sees himself mirrored in Laodice, but alone
nevertheless in his struggle against Rome and its satellites. Arsinoë
does not fight for Rome but for her son. Nevertheless, her interests coincide with those of Rome, and, more important still, so
do her weapons of ruse and stealth. *Nicomède* is thus a political

play about Rome, but even more a tragedy in which political machinations are defeated by contagious generosity.

Much about this struggle is familiar, particularly the solitude resulting from two worlds facing each other, unable or unwilling to understand each other. Arsinoë, like the Cléopatre of *Rodogune,* wants to rule men and through men. For this, she, a mediocre soul, must rely on other mediocre beings and cannot hope to win in a world of Nicomèdes she judges by her own standards. Understanding between the two is impossible: whereas Nicomède views others as human beings, Arsinoë, intent on "dazzling the King, Rome and the court" (346), moves by "artifice" (296) and treachery, and sees others as things to manipulate (337–38). Such plans must "abort" (1661), and though her son eventually will rule, he will hold the crown from Nicomède, and so, from Arsinoë's point of view, the plot has worked "for me, against myself" (1836). Whatever reconciliation there is at the end is less a surrender to opposing values than to hard evidence. The Machiavellian protagonists cannot believe that anyone would act with altruism. Nicomède is a loyal subject and repeatedly promises to remain so, but Prusias cannot trust a man he knows capable of rebellion. Nicomède does not get a chance to prove his sincerity until the end of the play, when the people demand that he be king. When he then allows his father to reign and forgives all those who plotted his downfall, he gives such proof as even the most cynical politicians must believe.

This raises another question: does their admiration mean eventual emulation? It is here that generalizations would be most dangerous, for they imply that the characters of *Nicomède* form two distinct camps. In fact, never before in Corneille has there been a demarcation line so difficult to trace. To be sure, there are obvious extremes, easy to categorize, such as Nicomède and Araspe, the villainous captain of the guards, but they are the exception.

The generosity of Nicomède is uncontaminated. When Prusias accuses him of duplicity, he cries out that not even his accuser believes that (1242). As far as he is concerned, "deceit is the game of petty souls . . . and of women" (1255–56). This remark is typical of his crushing irony which not unfrequently verges on the familiar—the realm of melodrama, and even comedy, but not of classical tragedy—and which makes the role so difficult to interpret, demanding familiarity without loss of dignity. Generosity translated into ironic sallies may be admirable but is far from perfect. Why does Nicomède always explain his position? Is it, as Octave Nadal suggests, to enjoy the radiance of his being, to make sure that he appears as dazzling as he is? [23] Whatever the reason, the result is that insolent posturing replaces action, whereas in men such as Rodrigue, the two had coexisted. Of course, as a dutiful son there is little that Nicomède could do, but even that little he does not attempt, and he is repeatedly saved by others less inclined than he to merely sneer at situations. First there is Flaminius, who decides to take him as hostage when Prusias has far more terrible options in mind (1609–10); then Attale, who leads the rebellion; and the people themselves, who worship Nicomède.

Nicomède is not the first passive hero of Corneille. Séleucus had rejected action and Suréna, Corneille's last creation, will do the same. But in both these cases inaction is the result of perception, of the destruction of the aura of mystery which Nietzsche saw as the sine qua non of action. Nicomède, on the other hand, lives in a world of illusion. He speaks like a man of action but does not act. He gives great lessons to all concerned but seems strangely unaware of what is going on around him, and Laodice repeatedly must warn him of his ineffectiveness (91–92, 967–70, and so on).

Laodice, for all her wisdom, is no less generous than her lover. She has one momentary lapse (1722), but it is brief and under the greatest stress. Interestingly enough it occurs when she believes Nicomède dead. This "fatal blow" has robbed her simultaneously of her beloved and her "respect and generosity." Could one speak then of a degree of generosity in the female predicated on the generosity of the male protagonist, a situation reminiscent of Chimène's "My generosity must equal yours"? Whatever the answer, Laodice's love and generosity are totally interdependent rather than at odds with each other as in so many of Corneille's plays. As a result, the moment that Laodice finds out that Nicomède is not dead, her fury is replaced by love, and generosity regains her soul. [24] The parallel with Chimène goes further. Laodice expects a lot of herself—more than did Chimène—since she is queen, and is jealous of her glory and her freedom, willing to accept as her rulers only "herself, reason, and the gods" (774). She never allows herself to forget that she is a queen (57) and that, as such, she can never stoop to marry a subject (65–66). Her problem in no way resembles that of the Infante, because she can hope that Nicomède will one day rule, and, putting her trust in his capabilities—"See to it that you are feared, and I will fear nothing" (98)—she finds the path to glory by admitting her love, while the Infante had found hers in painful silence.

If Laodice demands a lot of herself, she demands no less of Nicomède. If he is to keep her, he must be forever magnanimous and of a steady heart (1775–78). In accord with Corneille's optimism, such magnanimity must be rewarded, and Laodice, who is intent on maintaining her rank though she might lose her realm (786), eventually gets both. Nicomède voices the same sentiments when, taken as hostage and about to be shipped to Rome, he tells his father that he will be more king in Rome than Prusias in Bithynia (1386). By ending the play as he does, Corneille proves that such royal behavior deserves a royal theme.

Not all *généreux* in the play are as noble as the above. Attale, cowed by Rome—though never to the point of being base or devious (289, 1107, 1116, and so forth)—is fundamentally generous, and like so many of Corneille's secondary heroes, triumphs over his acquired traits in his "regeneration." Rome, however, has taught him some strangely ungenerous lessons. As a result, his attempts to win Laodice's hand with threats earn him some of the most devastatingly scornful comments of Laodice, and even more of Nicomède, who considers him a less than worthy rival (266). Fortunately, Nicomède's cruelly administered lessons do have an effect, and, as was the case after Laodice's momentary lapse (1744), generosity reenters his heart. Of paramount importance in this regeneration is his severance from Rome, which occurs when he becomes aware of its duplicity. But a question remains: is the regeneration complete or merely in his mind? He helps Nicomède, but by "outdeceiving" his mother. No true *généreux* (and certainly not Nicomède) would so stoop to conquer.

Flaminius never allows himself to forget that he is the ambassador of Rome, and even Nicomède admits that the job commands a certain behavior (1187–90). Though this may be argued, Flaminius construes the final outcome as being in the best interest of Rome (1849–50). As a result, Flaminius is motivated by a type of generosity that is tainted to say the least: "Perfect virtue needs prudence, and for its own sake, must take into consideration the times and places" (816–18). It is more involved with the facts of political life than with heroic integrity. This is perhaps why *Nicomède* never becomes a love story: in the struggle between heroism and politics there is no room for a luxury such as love. Rome's matrimonial plans for Laodice are prompted by nothing less than its fear of an excessively powerful ruler in Asia Minor.

Much the same is true if we look at the situation through the eyes of Arsinoë. Her path is not unlike that of Flaminius, but what is wise for him is selfish and base for her. There need be no lengthy analysis of her; her sisters-under-the-skin have been dealt with before. It must simply be pointed out that Arsinoë's fight for her son does not seem as disinterested as that of a mother like Marcelle. If Arsinoë wants Laodice as a wife for Attale, it is not the result of some maternal drive for a child's happiness but simply of her desire to extend her own power through him.

Once again, then, there is the old struggle between Machiavellian and *généreux,* with the former unable even to conceive of a generous attitude. Repeating the maxim of so many of her predecessors, Arsinoë states readily that there is no crime or deceit that is not legitimized by the throne it procures (291–92). Nicomède, purely generous, cannot act in a world of political intrigue. The *généreux* who do act infringe on their generosity by so doing, or rather by the methods used. The obvious failing of the play then, if it is meant to instill admiration for generosity, is that this generosity wins out in it only with the help of people willing to stoop to methods that are less than generous. Total generosity, such as Nicomède's, can only sneer and contemplate its own superiority. True, Nicomède ultimately gains a certain power to act and, like Auguste, pardons his foes to show that he has regained mastery over the situation as well as over himself, yet one cannot help but recall Médée's feeling of impotence in the unreal world that surrounded her, for, as has already been suggested, that final choice of Nicomède's is not really as free as it might at first seem.

In one respect, *Nicomède* does not so much innovate as carry an old Cornelian commonplace to its limit. In the early tragedies, there had been the passions and the pity of which the author spoke in the *Examen,* and there had also been a large dose of admiration resulting from the dazzlement mentioned earlier. In no play, tragedy or comedy, is this *éblouissement* more obvious, and admiration as patently *the* emotion elicited. As must be obvious, this had led Corneille into a dramatic impasse from which he would have to try and extricate himself.

IX   *Pertharite*

Having followed the impasse of pure admiration as far as he could, Corneille made an about face and devoted his next play to love. Whereas Nicomède-the-Generous crushed all other protagonists with his irony, it is ironic that in *Pertharite* the only character able to sustain our interest throughout the play is Garibalde, a Machiavellian counselor. *Pertharite*, like *Héraclius* and *Rodogune*, is a melodrama in which plot and drama are paramount, but with one exception: here, the psychological verities of the characters determine the action, rather than the obverse, as had been true in *Héraclius* and *Rodogune*. There is a catch to such a situation: should the protagonists begin to flounder the action ceases and the play disintegrates. To those who have already noted that Corneille frequently had problems sustaining a single coherent action over five acts, it will come as no surprise that *Pertharite* falls apart after the third act.

Grimoald, having risen to the throne of Lombardy because of the disappearance of Pertharite, now covets the latter's wife Rodélinde and neglects Eduige (Pertharite's sister) whom he once loved and who now loves him. When Rodélinde rejects the usurper, he tries to blackmail her by threatening to kill her son. She replies by accepting to marry him only if he kills that son with his own hands. When he hesitates, she offers to help him in the task. He accepts the challenge, but before it can be put into effect Pertharite reappears, changing the focus of the crisis. The struggle over identity is resolved when Grimoald, repentant, marries Eduige and rules over a part of the realm that Pertharite grants him.

Love predominates on all levels. Eduige loves Grimoald though she once rejected him because of his station. Grimoald loves Rodélinde but with a love not above suspicion: how much of it is pique, to spite Eduige, and how much of it is political, to secure his throne? Garibalde, Grimoald's Iago-like counselor, loves Eduige, but less than himself, the crown, and the "right to rule" (505–14). All in all, with Rodélinde's love turned to hatred, only Pertharite's love can be said to be above suspicion, but it invites pity rather than sympathy. This may be due in large part to the fact that in *Pertharite* love fights *vertu*. Pertharite is willing to give up his throne for the woman he loves, and Grimoald, although he knows what he must do, cannot readily give up his throne, because that also means giving up any hope of obtaining the woman he loves: "All my love is opposed to all my virtue" (1622). One of the many ironies of the play, and also one of its basic flaws, is that, to use Eduige's words, we are dealing with "strange kings" (346) who do not really know what they want. All the characters are imbued with a sort of erotic Machiavellism whereby all is fair in love's political war, and it blinds them all to the irony of the treadmill on which they waste their heroic efforts. To cite but one example, Grimoald loved Eduige; to be worthy of her and end her rejection he became king; now he can only reject her in turn and aim higher, to the queen; to be worthy of her he must not only be king but virtuous, and this virtue merely enhances her hatred. A further bit of irony can be seen in that, to rid himself of Eduige, Grimoald pushes Garibalde into her arms, the answer to all of Garibalde's scheming prayers. In Grimoald, the lover and the ruler are the reflections, one private, one public, of the same man, one who wishes to rule without tyranny but cannot do so on his own, a strangely anachronistic type of antihero.

The heroism of the later plays of Corneille is indeed difficult to define. It may well be that after Don Sanche and Nicomède there are no more purely heroic figures. The strongest and most consistent character of *Pertharite* is Garibalde. Selfish, he uses love and people to reach his goals, and he advises Grimoald to act as a tyrant only in the hope of seeing him fall victim of an uprising during which he might take his place. The irony is that he uses the very people who think they are using him, and such a situation exists only as long as the would-be users are Machiavellian, or at least ungenerous. The moment Grimoald becomes magnanimous Garibalde's plans fail, and he ceases to exist, dramatically as well as in fact.

The two protagonists then are Pertharite, the legitimate king, and Grimoald, the usurper. The full title of the play, *Pertharite, King of the Lombards*, helps to keep the play in proper perspective: Grimoald may have all the virtues, but he lacks legitimacy. Pertharite, on the other hand, although he has been shamefully defeated and has betrayed the very nature of royalty by renounc-

ing his throne for the sake of love, is the king.[25] Grimoald may be
virtuous, even generous, but he usurped the throne. As a result,
the greater he appears, the more the members of the royal family
—in particular Rodélinde—fear and hate him. A tyrant must look
and act like a tyrant if this world is to have any sense. Grimoald's
good fortune makes no more sense to Rodélinde than does the
attitude of Pertharite who accepts the status quo as the will of
Heaven. Interestingly enough, the end proves her to be right: her
offer to Grimoald, as monstrous as that of Rodogune, has the same
effect, that of forcing the interlocutor to examine himself and to
find himself. It is as a result of this examination as much as anything else that Grimoald sees the legitimacy of Pertharites' claim.

Pertharite, upon his return, is willing to yield the crown in exchange for the freedom of the woman he loves. This is not an
unconscious passion that speaks, but the very essence of kings. It
is this fundamental verity that confounds a Grimoald who has
examined himself, for that royal essence transcends the existence
wherein it is revealed.[26] Grimoald, in order to blind the people,
wanted not to recognize Pertharite (1823–24). When he finally
does, it is as a hero submitting to the superior synthesis of hero
and man that is Pertharite. Whatever the importance of love may
be in this play, its title confirms what the plot reveals: a definition
of royalty and the identification of the one true king. Pertharite,
in that final synthesis, saves his essence from the temporal and
succeeds in being, by tearing himself away from the eternal re-
creation that tormented Corneille's earlier heroes.[27]

It might be difficult to understand the total failure of *Pertharite*. It would seem that such generous and virtuous heroes could
carry the action for five acts without floundering. A look at the
heroines will help to understand the play's failure. In many of
the plays heretofore examined there are two women, one more
masculine than the other, each one acting as a frame of reference
for the other. *Pertharite*, in that respect, runs true to form. Eduige,
rejected by Grimoald who feel that he can discard that for which
he paid too dearly, tries to get Garibalde to serve her hatred. As
she puts it, the price of a scepter is to serve that hatred (395–96).
When Garibalde cleverly sees that she would hate him for killing
the man she still loves, and demands his reward first, she declares
that true love is never mercenary (483). But in view of her two
attempts to sell herself, of her wavering not only between two

men but between love and "the hatred of a brother" (324), the entirely unselfish devotion that she demands is preposterous.[28]

If Eduige is a poor standard-bearer for the feminine mystique, Rodélinde is a caricature of the masculine counterpart. She is torn between hatred and esteem for a man. Her hatred is a rational one which does not blind her to his qualities, just as love born of duty would not blind her to his faults (182–86). She admits that Grimoald reigns with love (174), and this is precisely what intensifies her inner struggle, since her hatred must equal her esteem (704), and it is in this framework that her monstrous proposition to the tyrant is explained: since she must admire Grimoald for his virtues, by forcing a murder on him she will force him to betray his latent tyrannical traits and dishonor himself. If he refuses she will perpetrate the deed herself and be dishonored, but either way crime will unite what too much virtue has kept apart (909–10). In either case, she will then be close enough to him to better seize the chance to kill him (985–98). This attitude, born of the demands of the Cornelian system, is completely devoid of any psychological realism. Even Médée had some regrets or reticence. Rodélinde seems almost gleeful at Grimoald's horrified reaction to her proposal. The rationale for her offer is understandable, but her ferocity is not. Seeking her glory in this inhuman fashion, she is frustrated by the return of her husband. Having declared that she did not lower herself "to weaknesses of women" (871), she proves it in her reunion with Pertharite by scorning feminine emotions (1411–14). When Pertharite suggests that harshness of glory should yield to the pursuit of happiness (1421–22), she attempts to assume a role that is not hers, and she thus fails, being forced to submit this glory to that of the men around her.

Eduige considers herself a "true lover" (1643); yet her past belies that statement. The same can be said of all the characters with the exception of Garibalde: they are seldom what they should be or claim to be. Grimoald in love is ungenerous and tyrannical precisely because he loves (1455–57), and Pertharite is quick to see that, were Rodélinde to give in to Grimoald, his virtues would again triumph (1458). In short, as André Stegmann has demonstrated, with Machiavellianism so close to winning the upper hand, heroism had to become inhuman and warped to unmask and defeat it. Viewed from that vantage point, *Pertharite* is the culmination of the "amoral logic of heroic sacrifice." [29] Unfortunately, amid characters devoted to self-interest, Rodélinde is the only one ready for that sacrifice. For three acts, she is central to the action. When the long-lost husband reappears, Rodélinde is forced to yield, and there is no one to take up the dramatic slack. Much of the interest of the play—and surely part of the blame for its failure—lies in Corneille's intellectual game whereby he posited some basic principles and then rigorously, logically (though with little regard for human psychology), let that machine run its course. All this might have produced a successful play but for the dramatic turn of events that confused the only character capable of furthering the action, and caused the play to fall apart.

Deservedly—despite some beautiful passages—the play failed, and Corneille admitted in the preface that it was perhaps time to retreat while the public still had good memories of him. Busying himself with the lucrative writing of religious literature, the good burgher retired, for the while, from the theater.

CHAPTER 5

The Last Flight of the Phoenix

I *Œdipe*

AS stated in the first chapter, Corneille's seven-year retreat was not solely one of pique and dejection. To be sure, the dismal failure of *Pertharite* must have affected the proud author, but the success of the *Imitation* must have consoled him no little. Nor did Corneille cave-in as far as theater was concerned. He rewrote his plays, penned three discourses on dramatic art and an *Examen* for each past play for the 1660 edition. Furthermore, as I have also pointed out, the length of this retreat can be overstated: illnesses, deaths in the family, and other personal problems consistently plagued the author; yet, as of 1656, a scant four years after *Pertharite,* he was back in harness, having accepted a commission to write a "machine" play, *La Toison d'or.* Before he could complete the task he became one of the protégés of Fouquet and asked his patron to name a topic with which he could prove that his once-damped genius had been revived by Fouquet's encouragement. Fouquet suggested three topics from which Corneille picked that of Oedipus, writing the play in two months.

Corneille had readily seen that the topic, perfect for antiquity, had many aspects that would not be accepted by the French of his day, particularly by the *précieux* and *précieuses* who gravitated around Fouquet. As a distraction from the atrocities of the legend (which would have offended the gentle souls in his audience), Corneille, as inventive as ever, introduced the two young lovers and in so doing removed Oedipus from his position of preeminence. As a further sop to the salon habitués, Corneille gave heroes and heroines an overly refined language that has dismayed the discriminating ever since. In spite of strong reservations by many critics, the play was a popular success, and the king added a large financial reward to the one already given the author by Fouquet. But in time the critics proved to be right, and the play was relegated to limbo. However, as the first tangible sign of Corneille's dramatic "renaissance" it is not without interest.

Œdipe has married Jocaste, widow of Laïus, and become king of Thebes. His stepdaughter, Dircé, and the prince of Athens, Thésée, are in love, but Œdipe has other plans for the young girl, not willing to let her marry a man of such stature as to make her powerful enough to dispute him over a throne that she believes to belong to her. A plague has been ravaging Thebes and the oracles have decreed that it will last until the death of Laïus has been redeemed in blood. Believing herself to be the only remaining offspring of Laïus, Dircé feels that it is up to her to offer herself as a sacrifice. Thésée, whose origin is somewhat obscure, offers himself as the possible long-lost son of Laïus. The truth is finally revealed: Phorbas, who was supposed to kill the infant son of Laïus, failed to do so, and Œdipe is that child, who has killed his father and married his mother. Œdipe blinds himself; Phorbas and Jocaste kill themselves; and Thésée and Dircé are left to find their long delayed happiness.

To the extent that the truth is revealed to Œdipe little by little; that each act ends in suspense, with frequently misleading clues; and that the following act frequently starts with something of a surprise, to that extent the play is well constructed. Unfortunately, as may be surmised from the synopsis, there is no unity of action in the play. Seven years after *Pertharite*, Corneille is back with the problem of legitimacy in government. But who would associate the legend of Oedipus with problems of political legality? To better see the difficulty brought on by this change in focus and by the additional digression of the young lovers it is necessary to first look at the characters created by Corneille.

Throughout the play Thésée and Dircé express their love in words and sighs to each other and to all concerned. Yet it is not an entirely reciprocal matter. Like Dircé, Thésée wants love to be sole master of its choice (166), but there the similarity ends. Never in a Cornelian tragedy has the heroic been so completely drowned out by the erotic. Thésée is ready to abandon everything for his love and feels that he could not live without Dircé who, like so many heroines before her, therefore feels obligated to give him a lesson in generous love: passion must elevate, not destroy heroes (67–70). Whereas Thésée's love is the great opponent of his generosity, that of Dircé is more along the lines traced in plays such as *Le Cid*, a further opportunity for self-assertion. Even her generous sacrifice is willed in part by her desire to prove her nobility as well as her love. This love, mired in temporal considerations, is as much an expression of self-interest as are Œdipe's political machinations. Her "pitiless thirst for glory" (779) makes her reproach her mother by refusing to understand how one might prefer love to glory (880), but as both Jocaste and Œdipe point out, that is excessive generosity (889, 956). Her refusal to make room in her heart for anyone but a king (495–96) and her narcissistic admiration of her willingness to sacrifice herself repeatedly infringe on the purity of her love, and one is tempted to agree with Octave Nadal's rather severe judgment of a young lady for whom the art of love is a consolation for not really loving.[1]

The character of Œdipe is even more complex. On the one hand we have an usurper standing in the way of a couple's happiness. On the other, there is the incestuous parricide. One of the basic flaws of the play is that these two do not coexist, but that the former predominates throughout the play, to be suddenly supplanted by the latter at the end. Having usurped Dircé's throne Œdipe does not know what to do with her. He cannot allow her to marry Thésée because, as Dircé readily sees (II, 2), to firm up his place on the throne he cannot have her married to a man strong enough to contest his claim and position. The reasons Œdipe gives for his refusal are all specious, and when the flaws of his arguments are pointed out he tries to act tyrannically: "I think I am king here," but the reply is right on target: "I know what you are, and it does not make me your subject" (421–24). That is Œdipe's first area of guilt: unlike Grimoald, he is consciously and deliberately tyrannical as well as usurper. Œdipe may be king by the will of the people as well as by marriage, but Dircé sees him as an usurper, and as *Pertharite* had already shown, in Corneille's canon, popularity has nothing to do with legitimacy. In this light Œdipe can only be viewed as a degenerated hero, guilty of the basest Machiavellian manipulation of hearts. As such, his importance is secondary, a hurdle to be overcome or removed. This could not be done without totally disregarding the Greek legend and the notion of a hero, however degenerated he might be.

To solve this problem Corneille shifted the focus back to the major ingredients of the legend. Dircé and Thésée, advocates of free will, see no excuse for regicide. Œdipe, on the contrary, sees himself as predestined to evil, an innocent tool of fate. To the end, even when he blinds himself, Œdipe proclaims his innocence, rejecting the guilt that is imposed on him and the fate that crushes him. The play then has two endings. The first one, to the love story, is a happy one in which the villain is removed, allowing the union of Thésée and Dircé. The second ending is unfortunate in that it is a denial, *in extremis,* of the entire political orientation of the play, prepared only by Thésée's speech on free will and by the public's foreknowledge of the legend. This second ending (1820–2010) is nevertheless a marvelous bit of tragedy in which Œdipe, guilty as a free agent, is now revealed as the tool of fate, innocent, regained to his *vertu* (1896) and to be pitied by all.[2] At this moment Dircé and her *galant* disappear before the grandeur of Œdipe. Whereas she sought self-immolation as a further proof of her purity (577–78) and of her generosity, Œdipe consummates his in order to triumph over the injustice of the gods. Transcending his destiny, Œdipe assures the triumph of his royal essence. Dircé may well hint of a future in which the gods will make things right (2010); Œdipe, by his act, has left that domain, challenging these unjust gods to prove the validity of their norms.

II *La Toison d'or*

Four years in the making, *La Toison d'or* had a magnificent début at the castle of the Marquis de Sourdéac, a wealthy eccentric who had commissioned it in 1656 and had been working on the machines himself since that time. Since the play's completion more or less coincided with the peace of the Pyrénées and the wedding of Louis XIV, Corneille and Sourdéac added a pompous prologue, with no connection to the action of the play, in which the events of the day were glowingly described. To further assure the success of the initial production Sourdéac imported the entire Marais troupe to his Normandy castle. He later gave them the machines so that they were able to stage an equally lavish production in Paris. Its success might have tempted Corneille into a new, lucrative, and popular career. Once again—as had been the case on the occasion of the success of *Andromède*—he chose not to, and this *pièce à machine*, like the first, must be considered as little more than a pleasant and profitable diversion.

And yet, the play is not without interest. Whereas the libretto for *Andromède* had been completely subjugated to the machines, the poem and stage effects of *La Toison* are complementary. However, the play was written to allow ample showing of dazzling stage effects and this emphasis, coupled with the exorbitant cost of such productions, doomed it.

Corneille called *La Toison* a tragedy, but its fickle lovers are more like those of his early comedies, relying on trickery and deceit (frequently in the form of affected sincerity that ill masks the real intent). The verbal gymnastics of Jason are more reminiscent of *L'Illusion comique* than of *Le Cid*. Throughout the play love is portrayed as omnipotent, with the heroic willingly sacrificed by the human. One of the aspects of this all-powerful passion is that it readily gives rise to its twin, hatred, a notion that brings to mind the plays of Racine. This love, which forever demands that reason be silenced (765, 1962–73, and particularly 1500–1501), is not a generous one, in any sense of the word. It wants to possess, to control, both in Hypsipyle, who cannot stand the thought of a happy rival (996–1003), or in Médée, who will not be bested and finds a perverse, "unequaled" joy in seeing her rival sacrificed to her (1567–79). In that, it is particularly interesting, because it is not only Racine that it prefigures, but Corneille's own concept as hinted at in some of the earlier plays and as fully elaborated in the upcoming ones.

Also of interest is the fact that this mythological fantasia, replete with tender declarations, is called a tragedy. Aaete, king of Colchos, voices some thoughts more pessimistic than any that Corneille had ever let a character of his express, but while they may suggest a new orientation for the author, it does not explain the label. By the same token, the elevated tone; the personages of consequence; dramatic confrontations such as the one between Hypsipyle and Médée in III, 4, during which Hypsipyle tries to cow her rival with "I am queen, madame, and crowned heads . . ." only to be cut short by Médée's "And I, I am Médée, and you bother me" (1330–31); all these are mere trappings of tragedy, and little more. If the label is at all to be justified, it is by focusing the attention on the potential, which is known through our foreknowledge of the legend and the prediction of Jupiter at the

end of the play. In this anachronistic sort of way, the Médée of
La Toison will find out what the Médée of *Médée* knows already,
namely, that her love will not serve her and that she will help-
lessly founder in Jason's world, only to be saved by a regained
generosity after a soul-searing—and thus cathartic—experience. At
the same time, the audience is warned of the shortcomings of
such a love, a warning that will serve well in the understanding of
Corneille's last plays. In the meanwhile, thanks to the dazzling
machinery of this fairy tale, our attention is diverted from this
tragic potential to the total fulfillment of the secondary characters.

III *Sertorius*

Having discharged his immediate obligations to his sponsors,
Corneille found himself once again immersed in the theatrical life,
ready to tackle a subject truly of his own choosing. It should not
surprise us that once again he chose to treat a moment of Roman
history, nor should it surprise us that, as in previous cases, the
history was little more than a starting point which he embroidered
and altered with all the powers of his inventiveness.

Stationed in Spain, Sertorius, Roman general allied to the rebel
Marius, has fallen in love with Viriate, queen of the Lusitanians.
Sylla, the Roman tyrant, has forced his general, Pompée, to renounce his wife Aristie and marry Emilie instead. For the sake of
the rebellion Sertorius decides to seek the hand of Aristie (who is
willing to thereby get her revenge) and allow his lieutenant, Perpenna, to woo Viriate. The news is suddenly spread that Emilie
is dead and Sylla has abdicated. All would now be in a position
to end well were it not for Sertorious' hesitations and misgivings
concerning the cause. Perpenna puts an end to that when, in a fit
of jealousy, he kills Sertorius. Pompée can only avenge his noble
foe and, reunited with Aristie, he grants Viriate freedom over
herself and her country.

Sertorius recalls *Horace* in many ways. It is a play dealing with
the evils of civil war. Alba and Rome were so close that much the
same may be said of Horace. Furthermore, each play is centered
on two parallel dramas—one public, one private. In *Sertorius*,
however, the divorce between Pompée and Aristie is repeated at
the state level between the tyrant and the rebellious forces. As
Aristie says, the two divisions are really one, and they have a com-

mon solution (1089). For all that, *Sertorious* comes much closer to *La Toison d'or* than to *Horace*.

As in the earlier play love must struggle in a political context, but whereas the love of Camille was a pure flame, such is not the case in *Sertorius*. Here, an imperfect love takes over. It may not fit the definition we normally give to love, but it is love just the same, and it is central to the action. Everything, the hesitations of Sertorius, the factionalism, even the death of the hero, are all directly attributable in part or in total to this strange love that makes Viriate esteem Sertorius more than she loves him; that allows Sertorius to waver, for politics's sake, between Viriate and Aristie; that sees Aristie willing to use Sertorious in her revenge against Sylla and Pompée, yet much happier to forgive and re-cal future—shades of Garibaldi! The irony of it all is enhanced by marry a man who had thought less of his love than of his politi-Perpenna who, in spite of his villainous role, is perhaps the only man truly in love.

This political love would leave the reader completely cold were it not for an occasional dropping of the mask: "Gods . . . what a cruel fate to love out of political reasons . . . when the heart is elsewhere" (369–72). As André Stegmann put it, Sertorius must choose between Viriate and Rome, between a tangible, legitimate, but selfish happiness, and the noble, altruistic sentiments which are, at best, hypothetical.[3] Caught between generous sterility and selfishness, Sertorious wearily melts into hesitation and inaction. If at first he leans toward self-sacrifice, events—and in particular the interview with Pompée—convince him that his stand may be very empty and senseless, and leading only to the unhappiness of the four principals. Once he dares reveal that truth to himself (1197–98), he also opens his heart to Viriate, declaring his love in one of the most touching scenes in all of Corneille (IV, 2). That scene is all the more touching because the tension between the protagonists is doubled by another one within each breast, which will be grasped more readily after a cursory look at the principals.

In *Sertorius* the confrontation between a "tender" and a "generous" woman is present again, but with a twist, in that both love, both claim to scorn love—though with quite dissimilar protestations—and neither one really succeeds. Aristie exaggerates in her rejection of love, which she leaves to "petty souls" (285–86), and immediately alerts the reader to her inherent eroticism. Viriate readily admits that she loves, but with a love that is not sensual and is solely attached to her "grandeur" (401–4). What she loves in Sertorius is his greatness, his merits, his omnipotence (405–12) and seeks in him, not a lover, but a husband. Whereas Viriate's dedication to her glory is manifest in every speech, Aristie's mask is seldom effective. Still in love with Pompée she cannot hide those feelings (1005–6), and if she plans to give herself to Sertorius it is precisely because of that love. In the past, we have seen Cornelian heroines willing to prostitute themselves to fulfill their duty. Aristie is willing to do that for her love. Viriate admits that she really knows neither how to love nor hate (1284), but these are the very motors of Aristie: "I have feelings, and depending on whether I am loved or hated, I love or hate in turn, and my glory sustains my hatred and my love" (994–96). Having lost one title when Pompée rejected her, she must have another no matter how many heads such a quest might cost (1126). Viriate, on the other hand, has feelings for Sertorius, but they are "a gift of her glory, not of her heart" (1285–86). In fact, she readily admits that "love is not what presses me" (1390). Aristie, seeking only revenge out of love, readily abandons that quest and forces her heart to forget past miseries (1888) when happiness beckons. Viriate, having lost the man she saw as a noble consort, can only accept the peace that is offered (1889) and forever renounce both war and marriage.

Sertorius tries hard to be like Viriate and not have to consult his senses, but he loves, "and perhaps more than anyone has ever loved," and the more he tries to fight that love the more it reveals his weakness to him (1195–98). This love gains much of its relative strength from the nature of Sertorius's generosity, which exists more in word than in deed. Rome being what it is has become a mere physical enclosure (929), while Sertorius, surrounded by all those who represent the essence of Rome, has become the center of things: "Rome is no longer in Rome, it is where I am" (936). In the words of Judd Hubert, Sertorius, "the greatest Roman of them all," has become "the moral center of the universe." [4] It is precisely for this reason that Viriate wants to make of "a great Roman, . . . a great king" (1383), and it is precisely for that reason that Sertorius, like Pertharite, cannot abdicate his essential valor: men such as he cannot have any effective masters, nor can they surrender their leadership (953–55). He is thus thrown into a "quandary from which only Perpenna's dire deed can extricate him." [5]

And yet, while publicly Sertorius may be the "greatest Roman of them all," the private man is selfish and stubborn. In the great debate with Pompée, when the latter demonstrates the near impossibility of attributing right to any side in a civil war, Sertorius does not even hear the arguments he refutes: the general unhappiness that he may cause does not seem to concern him at all, only the idea to which he sacrifices everything. His "I am the only one left . . ." (1458), a sort of "everyone is wrong but I," is more ludicrous than heroic. To make matters worse, Sertorius is simultaneously uncompromising and indecisive. He delays, hesitates, and before he can decide, that decision has been removed from him: Sylla having abdicated and Emilie having died, Pompée and Aristie are reunited. Shortly thereafter, and before Sertorius can "reactivate" his heroism, Perpenna kills him.

Not only is Sertorius willing to sacrifice the general happiness of everyone to his idea, but it is a vain sacrifice, since we know from the start that Perpenna will not put up with all this and will kill him. As a result, we are somewhat detached from a situation which otherwise comes as close to being truly tragic as any that Corneille had tried in years. Whereas in past plays the general happiness at the end of the play makes us forget some secondary "tragedy," here the fortune of Pompée, of Aristie, and of Rome do little to diminish the pathos of the tragic couple that was Sertorius and Viriate, the former shamefully assassinated, the latter doomed to a solitary life on a now meaningless throne. [6]

Sertorius is much more than a play of superfluous sacrifices, of Roman grandeur, or of heroic masks. The numerous attempts to reconcile the private and the public sectors always fail, and Sertorius' assertion that Rome is where he is (936) is followed by the voicing of his sweetest hope—that of seeing Rome once more (1359). This last confession only confirms the earlier one that, though Roman, he is nonetheless a man (1194). What we are witnessing here is more than mere sentimentality; it is the basic affectation of a hero in spite of himself, and in spite of his age (1196). This fall marks the destruction of the hero, of all that is temporal, a destruction that was necessary for the birth of something new. Not that we have already a synthesis of any sorts here:

none is possible, not because Sertorius will be assassinated too soon,[7] but rather because he refuses to be involved in either heroism or sentimentality. Sertorius, as his last speech indicates, is a tired and troubled hero, prefiguring Suréna. But Suréna, despite his weariness, is capable of will. The synthesis of which I spoke earlier demands an effort of will which Sertorius, a resigned old man, will not make. But the idea is there, and Corneille will shortly bring it to fruition.

IV *Sophonisbe*

If in *Sertorius* we see the decline of the hero, we are witness to his complete demolition in *Sophonisbe*. In 1634 Mairet had gotten one of his greatest successes with a *Sophonisbe* that was still being played in 1663 when Corneille presented his. The critics, from the first day to our time, have enjoyed the obvious comparisons, and it is very possible that Corneille wrote his play to invite such comparison, rejecting those aspects of Roman history that Mairet had kept reintroducing those Mairet had rejected. Be that as it may, the critics have been unanimous on only one point: namely, neither play is very good.

Sophonisbe, a Carthaginian queen, had married Syphax for purely political reasons, having been previously engaged to Massinisse, a king of Numidia allied to Rome. When Massinisse defeats Syphax, Sophonisbe willingly marries him, but again without love. To complicate matters, Corneille invented Eryxe, queen of Getulia, who once saved Massinisse, fell deeply in love with him, and is now a prisoner, along with Syphax and Sophonisbe, in the Roman camp. Scornfully rejected by Sophonisbe, Syphax warns the Romans against her scheming nature. Summoned to appear before Scipio, Sophonisbe asks her husband to spare her this shame. Instead, he advises her to use her charms on Scipio. She refuses and, as a last resort, he sends her a poison, but she disdains it, taking one of her own, while Lelius, the Roman consul, voices hope for Eryxe's future happiness.

Once again, Corneille had created a work in which two women face each other to voice their hatred and defend their attitudes. The best scenes of the play are those in which Eryxe and Sophonisbe flail each other verbally in confrontations that frequently verge on the vulgar yet come equally close to the dramatically sublime.

Sophonisbe, as Corneille himself stated in the prefatory letter, has "a little love, but reigns over it," sacrificing it to her hatred of Rome. Rejecting Syphax, an old man who has survived defeat, Sophonisbe asserts her ability to live and die like a queen (384). Only half of that is proven by her suicide. She is a very complex character, constantly contradicting herself in a search for self-justification. In spite of repeated indications that her whole life is predicated on patriotism, she seems motivated more often than not by jealousy (1546–47), her greatest pleasure coming from seeing a defeated rival (711–14).

Nor should this jealousy be seen as closely tied to a normal erotic reaction. Whatever love Sophonisbe may feel, whatever patriotism she may voice, are but masks for one of the most selfish creatures in all Corneille. She surrenders to power, not to love (968), yet with the hope of finding a new ally for her country. If Massinisse is "all hers," he will also belong entirely to Carthage (718). But we have every right to question the chauvinism of Sophonisbe. When Eryxe argues for peace, Sophonisbe demands a continuation of war at all costs to herself, her husband Syphax, and all of her country. When Syphax worries about what might happen should he die, she responds with typical cynicism that what happens to her after his death is none of his business (381–82). The basic problem with this totally unsympathetic character is that for her, as for the old Sertorius, the word "glory" is abused, given credit for motives that are more in the domain of self-interest, pride, and political ambition. As André Stegmann put it, she has all the stiffness of the 1640 heroism, minus the enthusiasm, but compounded by cynicism,[8] a damnable combination that shuts off any feeling the audience might have for her.

Eryxe is tender but no less proud, and she is at least as generous. With a quiet sense of decorum, she is proud of a heart that is steadfast regardless of the fickleness of others (1650, 1820–21), an interesting foretaste of Bérénice. However quiet and modest she may be, she has tremendous courage, rising to defend her dead rival whose death, in her eyes, shames Rome (1810). She readily defies Rome to assert her mastery over her own being (1820). Rejected, she feigns not to love and claims to consider only the royal position in Massinisse, but that claim ends with an allusion to her rival that leaves little doubt about her real feelings (897–916). When she puts down the mask we see her as she truly is, a beautiful woman who wants to be loved freely—"Of what good is a hand forced by duty" (480)—and will not have a union of state: "I love Massinisse, and expect him to love me:/ I adore him, and want him to adore me as much,/ And for me marriage to him would be a long trial,/ If he were not all mine, as I all his" (499–502). It is this truly generous attitude which more than anything else condemns the self-indulging Sophonisbe.

Unfortunately, the other protagonists suggest little more than a tired rehash of *Nicomède*. Syphax is old and weary of war and of a love he calls an "imbecile slavery" (1193). Although described in a manner to elicit sympathy, that feeling is supplanted by pity when his cruel wife mocks him in defeat and by scorn when the jealous old man betrays her to the Romans. Massinisse is the most unheroic of kings to date. He allows Sophonisbe to insult him and the Romans to insult her. Sophonisbe, about to die, "gives him back" to Eryxe and proudly claims to be the cause of his degeneration (1659–66), but here again she is blinded by her own vanity. Earlier, she had few illusions about him (1580–81). His love is obviously little more than pique because Eryxe did not show all the warmth he expected when they met, and neither of the two women think much either of his power over his passions or of his capability for fidelity. Corneille, by inventing an ending to the play in which, after all the Romans do to his wife, Massinisse not only refuses to follow her in death but continues in their service, was anything but equivocal on that matter.

The interest of the play, as far as the modern reader is concerned, rests then solely on a few dramatic confrontations and on prefigurations of some great characters to come. Otherwise, the political discussions, the Machiavellian machinations and patriotic debates, are intellectual games which, considering the petty souls involved, cannot elicit the attention they did in *Horace* or *Nicomède*. Eryxe is apolitical, Africa is mediocre at best, and Rome, that Rome we have seen since *Nicomède,* is glibly Machiavellian, playing with human lives and hearts. Considering the hearts it plays with—it is difficult to feel much sorrow for an Eryxe that will settle for a nonentity such as Massinisse—who cares?

V *Othon*

In the preceding plays Corneille had elaborated several notions which were to remain as part of his dramaturgy for the rest
of his life, and it is undoubtedly because they are so foreign to
the overt heroism of the early tragedies that these late plays are
usually swept under the academic and critical rug. I do not wish
to imply that these are all great plays worthy of a place in the
active repertoire of the Comédie Française, but many of them are
worthy of close study, if only for the light that they shed on the
various concepts Corneille was trying to evolve. In many ways
Othon is the logical successor of *Sophonisbe,* with some aspects
enhanced, others softened, the differences showing Corneille's
hesitations, his groping for a path that would eventually lead to
Suréna.

As Corneille stated in the dedicatory letter, there had never
been a play in which so many marriages are proposed without
any being concluded. He might have added that he had never
analyzed so keenly the absurdity of politics based on personal
human relationships. Nor had he ever complicated to such an extent a basically simple situation in order to show not only this
absurdity, but the added one of a ruler surrounded by self-seeking advisors, all uttering equally valid—and therefore equally
invalid—yet contradictory verities, a situation that could only result in the destruction of stability, of norms, of all that a hero can
cling to. In such a climate, reminiscent of *Pompée,* of *Sertorius,*
and of *Sophonisbe,* a hero has no choice but to abdicate and submit to the exigencies of the moment, sacrificing either the glory
of the public being or the happiness of the private one, or both.

The basic issue of *Othon* is quite simple: two people in love
sacrifice their happiness for political expediency in what is eventually revealed to be a black comedy of errors and an exercise in
futility. The actual plot of the play is so involved as to defy proper
summarization, but the main ideas are the following: Galba, the
Roman emperor, has three advisers, Vinius, Lacus, and Martian,
the latter a freedman. Othon, a senator, loves Plautine (the daughter of Vinius) and therefore discourages Camille (the niece of
the emperor) who loves him. Galba being an old man, the question of an heir is raised, and in this cruel world of political
machinations the matter of candidacy is also a matter of life and

death. Vinius therefore asks Othon to give up Plautine and woo Camille so that he may have a better chance to rule. Plautine readily makes the sacrifice, priding herself on having loved a man worthy of the throne, but more probably motivated by the thought of wanting to save Othon's life. All this is in vain when Galba decrees that Othon will wed Camille, but that the throne will go to Plautine who will marry Pison. Othon, his life threatened, leaves Rome, but is elected emperor by the praetorian guards who kill Pison. Othon returns to Rome where Galba and Vinius are killed by Lacus, and Plautine, while mourning her father, allows Othon to hope for a future marriage.

For once, there is no struggle between generous and Machiavellian protagonists, every character belonging, in varying degrees, to the latter category. Everyone wears a mask for public viewing; unfortunately, it is never a heroic one, merely one of expediency. Most obvious of these masks are those worn by the three advisers of Galba. Never had Corneille given so clear an argument for personal reign without ministers, bad advisers, factionalists, or usurpers. It is a cerebral argument, legalistic, logical, inexorably drawing the admiration of the public; unfortunately, the heart has little place in it.[9]

Galba's counselors are as vile as any in Corneille, fully as despicable as those of *Pompée*, so low as to be unworthy of contradiction (1704), moved solely by self-interest, and doomed to destroy each other. Martian is a "vile slave"; Vinius a double-dealing mediocrity who advises his daughter to "love Othon, . . . but love yourself more" and to reign with whoever will reign (1323–28); and Lacus a terrifying Iago who, when killing his master, calls the blows a "last hommage" to the emperor's glory (1788–90). It is this demonic triumvirate that makes a heroic stance suicidal: a ruler left to his own devices and moved by his inherent generosity will know how to recognize merit; but when advisers motivated by selfishness have his ear, noble people are at their mercy. This is the conclusion reached very early in the play (24–30) by Othon who, more human than a Rodrigue, decides to play the game in order to survive.

Whereas Vinius equates glory with freedom, or even power, Othon sees it as the early heroes did, both in love and in politics. Unfortunately, he yields to the realities of life, and, in a move that Rodrigue could only have called perfidious, he courts Camille, just as Plautine will fail by consenting to marry Martian. Othon's attachment to Plautine, like Pauline's to Polyeucte, has undergone a metamorphosis: born of self-serving motives it is now true love, and its sacrifice is all the more bitter because it is made futile by Galba's change of heart which gives Othon to Camille and the throne to Plautine.

Othon may be the titular character of the play, but here again, as in so many previous instances, the best scenes belong to the women. This does not mean that *Othon* was mistitled. It is after all a play dealing with a political struggle from which Othon emerges victorious. However, no matter how brilliantly that plot may be presented, it does not move. The love element is perfectly balanced, Othon and Plautine in love with each other, the matter complicated by Camille loving Othon and Martian loving Plautine. That balance, however, does not go beyond the basic a priori. Verbally, Othon is too much the senator, and his declarations of love are harangues in which the women believe only because they want to. And so, once again, it is to the women that one must turn to find the dramatic gems of the play.[10]

For Camille the interests of the State and of her heart seem to coincide until Galba's fateful decision. When she then sees both love and the crown escape her, she refuses at first to listen to reason, believing only her optimistic heart (829–32), but when Othon's failings become manifest she rejects him coldly, clinching her arguments with a beautiful line: "You only love the Empire, and I loved only you" (1144). The past tense of the second hemistich, striking home, foreshadows the declaration with which she ends the fourth act: "If the return from wrath to love is sweet, one easily passes back from love to wrath" (1487–88).

Plautine finds her happiness in a love which aspires only to "love and be loved" (316). She sees—as Chimène and Rodrigue had seen before and as Bérénice will see shortly—that pure love can survive in spite of physical barriers that may spring up. Surrendering all hopes for physical happiness, she bases her felicity on the knowledge that she acted out of love for a man worthy of being emperor. Such a sacrifice is nevertheless quite painful, and when Camille decides to rub salt into the wound, dramatic fireworks erupt.

Such a scene is the fourth one of Act IV. Camille, deeply unhappy, comes to gloat over the even greater misery of Plautine, unaware that Plautine is armed with the knowledge that she is loved. In a vitriolic exchange, the would-be victim becomes the torturer, as André Stegmann puts it,[11] particularly when she points out that Othon gave himself to one, sold himself to the other (1376). Camille gets her revenge in the next act: Othon is believed dead; Galba cynically tells Plautine not to mourn him and to consider only the hated Martian, whom he now destines her to marry. Camille cannot resist the temptation and sarcastically remarks, as she leaves the stage, that three is a crowd when lovers wish to talk (1682). Such a revenge can, of course, only be temporary. Just as providence operated against the bad advisors, so does it work its magic to resolve the problems of the lovers: Plautine, self-effacing for the sake of her love, may look forward to total fulfillment whereas Camille will have to settle for friendship (1832).

And yet, in the end, Plautine's victory is anything but total. The flawed (though deeply human) hero returning as an "unfortunate lover" (1807) to claim the throne finds that it has cost perhaps more than it was worth, and Corneille, urged by his incorrigible optmism, ends the play with one of these contrived *dénouements* which suggest that happiness may yet be around the corner. The problem with such an ending is that it, like Othon's original sacrifice, is superfluous. In this tragedy of love sacrificed to politics, Plautine—and to a lesser extent Othon—has seen that only an abstraction sheltered in the human heart can survive in a world of contingencies. To effectuate that salvation, she has had to offer herself in a most painful sacrifice. It is in the description of that sacrifice, in the portrayal of people hurting each other to make up for their own hurt, that Corneille comes closest to the Aristotelian concept of tragedy. The contrived ending of *Othon* has no place in that world.

VI *Agésilas*

Continuing the trend of applying new twists to tried methods, Corneille next penned *Agésilas,* a heroic comedy despite its being called a tragedy. Of the political tragedy it retains the insistent apology of personal reign, the momentous decisions, the dangerous decisions, but little else. Ever in search of new ways of demonstrating his inventive powers, the sixty-year-old Corneille decided to abandon the isometric alexandrine form of tragedy, intermixing octosyllabic lines with the alexandrines. Corneille was thus hoping to achieve a more prosaic tone as advocated by Aristotle. The resulting free verse [12] is indeed prosaic and is equally undramatic. To make matters worse, there is no connection between changes of mood and changes in meter, and the frequent lapses into bantering make the play more akin to the tender pastorals that had once been popular than to the great tragedies of Corneille. If this was an attempt to rival the successes of the lyric plays of Quinault and of Pierre's brother Thomas, it failed pitifully, and the murmurs heard after *Othon* became even louder after *Agésilas.*

Lysander, a Spartan general, has two daughters, Aglatide, engaged to the Persian Spidridate, and Elpinice, engaged to Cotys, king of Paphlagonia. However, Elpinice loves and is loved by Spidridate, while her ambitious sister would gladly take Cotys, if only because he is a king. Cotys, to complicate matters, loves neither sister, preferring the sister of Spidridate, Mandane, who is also loved by Agésilas, the king of Sparta. Cotys suggests a deal to Spidridate when Agésilas, jealous, tries to force himself on Mandane and refuses to allow others to be happy if he cannot. In the meanwhile Agésilas has discovered a plot by Lysander but, like *Cinna's* Auguste, he forgives and even gives up Mandane. As a result Spidridate will marry Elpinice; Cotys, Mandane; and Agésilas, Aglatide.

As can readily be surmised from the above, the plot is complex, with many meanderings, yet a sense of irrevocable logic pervades the entire play. The suspense is slowly built up until Act III, when Agésilas meets his rival in love (Cotys) and in politics (Lysander), each confrontation a dramatic scene, well prepared, and followed by a scene of introspective speculation during which the mind of Agésilas is beautifully revealed. One may readily sense impending tragedy in each of these scenes, but that tragedy is never realized, and *Agésilas* is more akin to Corneille's own comedies of intrigue than to any other genre. This is not only a matter of form or language, a language which, by the way, has many lapses; it is also, and foremost, a matter of the attitudes of the protagonists.

Marriage in *Agésilas* is as much a political tool as it was in the starkest political plays, and the question of personal rule as opposed to the rule of a minister is certainly not new. And yet, all these considerations are secondary to love as a prime mover, a love that is not the usual result of esteem, but a "blind sympathy" independent of merit and will (542–46). With the exception of old Lysander, everyone in this play is in love, yet willing to submit to the exigencies of glory, duty, or honor. At first glance the acts of submission seem very diverse: Aglatide will obey her father yet would prefer to remain single if she cannot marry a king (807–9); Elpinice will also obey, in spite of her reluctance to sacrifice pure love; Mandane, less ambitious than Aglatide but more so than Elpinice, would willingly submit to either Cotys or Agésilas, since both are kings. Underneath all these masks the characters bear a striking resemblance to each other. Aglatide may well declare that as long as a lover is a king, he is only too lovable in her eyes (126–27); she may readily assume a happy-go-lucky mien rather than pine for the impossible (1555–56); all that banter is merely a mask that allows her to keep her dignity intact when the inner person is crying out against a most painful sacrifice.

I have just stated that everyone submitted. That is not quite true, for if it were so the play would end in absurd and universal unhappiness. As it is, Cotys refuses to yield, and it is he who thus forces the issue as a result of which Agésilas conquers himself. This is not by any means a tragic self-immolation. Agésilas does not sacrifice a great love, but an infatuation, and through his move, dictated by generosity, he simultaneously recovers his kingly essence and the noblest, most generous of the three women, whom he once loved. As a result of this *dénouement* (taken in the most literal sense of the word), there is a perfect assortment of lovers, the degree of noble ambition in each woman determining the position of the man that she obtains. Unfortunately, in view of the mood that prevails, *Agésilas* not only denies the label of tragedy, it even belies the notion of heroic comedy. *Othon* only tried to destroy heroism. *Agésilas* mocks and degrades it.

VII *Attila*

Après l'Agésilas,
Hélas!
Mais après l'Attila,
Holà.
(After *Agésilas*, alas! But after *Attila*, stop.)

An earlier version of this poem by Boileau simply read: "I have seen *Agésilas*, alas," so there can be no doubt as to the meaning of the first two lines. Critics have been debating the meaning of the last two since their publication. Did Boileau want Corneille or his critics to stop? *Agésilas* had been a total failure; *Attila* had a respectable success. In many ways *Attila* repeats the lessons of the previous political tragedies, and many a spectator or reader must have felt that the point had been made sufficiently well without any need for further belaboring; on the other hand the play presents some rather novel variations on the old themes. The question then is not what Boileau meant by his *"holà"* but whether the play has any merits, intrinsic or to the student of Corneille in general.

In order to control two powerful nations, Attila has asked in marriage both Ildione, sister of the Frankish king, and Honorie, sister of the Roman emperor, intending to marry one and keep the other hostage. He also has in his power two kings, Ardaric (who loves and is loved by Ildione) and Valamir (who loves and is loved by Honorie). Attila is torn between the woman he loves (Ildione) and the one who will give him the greatest political power (Honorie). To that dilemma is added the fact that to reject one of the princesses means the alienation of a nation. To avoid this pitfall, Attila asks the two vassal kings to see to it that one of the women rejects him. When they fail, he tries himself, only to succeed too well, Ildione rejecting him because he requested it, Honorie because she will not have a man rejected by her rival. When Attila finds out that the two women love his vassals, he sets the kings against each other, promising deceitfully that the victor shall have his mistresses. The impending tragedy is preempted by Ildione, who agrees to marry Attila, intending to kill him on the wedding night, but a hemorrhage strikes down the tyrant before he reaches the altar.

Is this just another play setting love against politics? Just another debate between the advocates of Machiavellism and generosity? Not quite. For one thing, the days of Machiavellian counselors seem to be gone, and Octar, Attila's confidant, is colorless and of no consequence. Furthermore, Attila is too wrapped up in his love to be truly astute, and no one in this play is really generous. Nor are we dealing with the struggle between a tyrant and legitimate rulers. If a single political question predominates, it is one dealing with the very definition of royal essence, one raised by the women of the play, and to which neither Attila, a *parvenu*, nor the two vassals [13] can supply a proper answer.

Attila is wily without being astute, forceful yet hesitant, a sentimental politician whose perverse notions prevent him from even becoming an effective scourge of God. As one critic puts it, even his cruelty is a "pitiful weakness." [14] Cynically proud of his vices and crimes he considers insults superfluous and sweet (1571–72), since they prove only that he is capable of "always being Attila" (1564). There have been such monsters before in Corneille, yet Attila adds a new dimension to the old form. New is the volatile character that causes rapid changes in mood, from unctuous gallantry to barbaric self-assertion, ruled in turn by the shrewdest of minds and the most instinctive of hearts, by his erotic and his political thirsts. Wanting to keep the best of two worlds, he is torn between the woman he loves and the one most likely to get his immediate power. Like all the characters of Corneille, he constantly refers to his glory, but in his mouth and mind that word becomes synonymous with "empire." Perhaps better than ever before, Corneille here shows us a human heart prey to a fundamental inner split. Attila wants power; his love is in his way. More important still, he wants to be master of himself, and the beloved is forever infringing on that autonomy, being simultaneously "cruel poison of the soul, and sweet charm of the eyes" (764). For the sake of his integrity he must fight off this "poison," the woman he loves. A calm Sertorius, even a gentlemanly Agésilas could do this; a volatile, elemental Attila cannot.

Attila is by no means the only one failing to reach heroic dimensions. Valamir, as Honorie constantly reminds him, is not much of a king any more. Ardaric, like Ildione, is too much in love to consider the demands of his royal essence, and all the political noises made by that loving couple are strictly to safeguard their love.

As for the two princesses, they are again paired off, one proud, one tender. Viewed solely in the context of *Attila*, they are extremely well presented and are dramatically viable. However, it is very difficult for the reader to forget that he has already seen such a couple quite a number of times, and the result is that their position seems frozen and conventional. This is unfortunate, for there is a subtle progression in the presentation of these couples, one that must be perceived if the later plays are to be fully appreciated as the culmination of a great career.

Honorie loves Valamir, but refuses a king "forced to obey" (420) because her glory has demands as great as her love (443). Promised in marriage to Attila, she fears his choice: if he accepts her, she must relinquish Valamir; if he rejects her, her glory will not have been the equal of her rival's beauty (982). The only possible solution is to forestall Attila's decision by leaving with Valamir (475–76), a solution that has a prerequisite, Valamir's recovery of his royal essence: "I want a king: see if you are one" (490).

Ildione is Honorie's reluctant rival. She cannot refuse Attila, yet has no intention of volunteering herself. (Her reconquest of Attila, near the end of the play, is solely to save Ardaric, and not even Attila is fooled by that stratagem.) Though she knows her duty is to accept, she fervently hopes that Attila will reject her (625–26). Furthermore, she admits her love far more readily than Honorie, and that love is ready for any sacrifice, be it of modesty (671–72) or of her entire happiness, as when she offers herself to Attila. She repeatedly tries to assume a more vigorous posture, but every attempt fails, her last one ending in a complete surrender to "natural tenderness and timidity" (1447–48).

Both women consistently speak the language of generosity, a mask in either case. There the similarity ends. Ildione wears that mask for the sake of a love so selfless as to allow her to sacrifice everything to it. Honorie is no more generous than she is in love. As far as she is concerned, both are mere tools to serve her jealousy, her thirst for vengeance, and her general egomania. Honorie repeatedly attempts to use others to obtain a type of glory which she cannot obtain on her own. On the other hand, Ildione sees her happiness on a completely different plane and is ever ready to sacrifice herself for the love she shares with Ardaric. As a result the death of Attila affects the two women quite differently: with the obstacle removed, Ildione will live happily ever after with the man she loves; Honorie, doomed to remain on her treadmill of self-aggrandizement, the impotent victim of her own definition of glory, can only assure her lover that their problems are just beginning and that "our altered destinies have in no way changed my heart" (1788).

Attila's fatal hemorrhage, though historically justified, is yet another deus ex machina through which Corneille allowed divine justice to prevail. To be sure, it has been universally predicted, and the public has been well prepared. Just the same it is a convention that Corneille abused, an unnatural opening in a dramatic impasse, and a flaw without a doubt. However, with or without that flaw, *Attila* has been relegated to dramatic limbo, and if it deserves to be rescued from it, it is not as a viable entity but because better than any other play of Corneille it unites what André Stegmann has called the old providential view of history and a new psychology in which heroism is no longer anything more than the defense of a legitimate love against the infringements of an absurd or abusive policy.[15]

VIII   *Tite et Bérénice*

Shortly after *Attila*, all Paris applauded Racine's *Andromaque*, and even Corneille's most avid admirers had to admit that a new kind of French tragedy had been born. *Andromaque* had a success such as Corneille had never obtained, and it was even played at the Louvre, in the Queen's apartment, an honor never bestowed on Corneille. There can be no doubt that Corneille felt the need to reassert his talent in the face of his rival's success, but it was not until 1670 that he produced another play.

Several legends have sprung up about the two author's almost simultaneous treatment of the same theme. Some say that Henrietta of England gave the subject of Titus and Berenice to both authors. Others suggest that only Racine was commissioned and that Corneille, trying to show that he was still alive, decided to scoop his younger rival. Be that as it may, both poets worked feverishly, and Racine's *Bérénice* preceded Corneille's *Tite et Bérénice* by eight days on stage and by ten in print. The subject is basically a political one that should have allowed Corneille every hope of outdoing his young rival, but such was not the case. While Corneille wrote another good political play, Racine created a masterpiece of delicacy and tenderness. *Bérénice* was played for thirty days without interruption, has been frequently reactivated, and is still being played today; *Tite et Bérénice*'s first run was uninterrupted for only eight days, died fairly quickly, and has not been played since 1683, the victim of a comparison that is deplorable because—while *Tite et Bérénice* may not be as great as *Bérénice*—it is nevertheless a most creditable play. Some critics have suggested that it should be revived to allow comparisons; I would suggest a revival for the sake of the play's own merits.

Throughout the play Corneille manages the suspense admirably, and there is constant tension; yet the plot is very simple showing, if nothing else, that Corneille's love of complications has frequently been overstated, at least as far as *Tite et Bérénice* is concerned. Domitie and Domitian are in love, but her ambition makes Domitie prefer Domitian's brother Tite, who loves Bérénice, a Jewish queen. A Roman law, however, prohibits such a marriage to a foreign queen, and Tite is on the verge of abdicating all rights to the throne when Bérénice convinces him that this is not a proper solution. The Senate, urged by Domitian's friends, declares itself in favor of the union, but Bérénice renounces her newly found happiness to forestall the misfortunes bound to result from a marriage distasteful to Rome, and the play ends with this renunciation, Tite forsaking any other possible marriage and vowing to remain forever true to their love, the sadness of the moment mitigated slightly by the thought that Domitian will eventually inherit the throne and thus be able to find happiness with Domitie.

Corneille considered his play a *comédie héroïque* because neither state nor life is ever at stake. Racine called *Bérénice* a tragedy, rejecting Corneille's criteria and asserting the need only of a momentous action, heroic participants, aroused passions, the whole imbued with "that majestic sadness which is all the pleasure of tragedy." This credo, stated in the preface to *Bérénice,* would force any reader of *Tite et Bérénice* to label it a tragedy also, though the last ingredient, the all-important "majestic sadness," is hard to find in the first four acts.

The play is well structured, and each one of these first four acts contributes to the elaboration of a political situation within which a human quartet interacts. That is perhaps the reason for the play's strength, and its weakness. Never in all Corneille have the private and public beings been at greater odds, and for four acts we see all the possible variations on public posturing only to find ourselves, at the last moment, face to face with the private individuals bereft of pretense, stripped of heroism, in all their touching humanity. For four acts *Tite et Bérénice* is a political play; the fifth act is simultaneously a betrayal of the first four and as powerful a resolution of personal drama as Corneille had penned to date. The political drama is self-evident and needs no further elucidation. The four protagonists, as posturing public figures and suffering individuals, deserve a closer look.

If one wishes to see in *Tite et Bérénice* the continuation of the trend away from the heroic, there is no need to look beyond Domitian. Devoid of heroism, and even of civic pride, Domitian considers himself a pure lover who "sees, hears, believes only his love" (340). At times little more than a precious gallant, he is nevertheless capable of great passion. Unfortunately it is at these moments, when he might otherwise deserve our sympathy, that he shows his selfishness and his degradation by resorting to any means to obtain the object of his desires. He cruelly declares to Domitie that he will love Bérénice just to hurt Domitie (1264); he reminds Tite that Domitie may marry him but never love him; and he is quite willing to hurt Rome by influencing the Senate into voting against its interests, just so that he can marry Domitie.

Tite has not allowed himself to be as "degenerated" as his brother, though he too is a prisoner of love. The distance traveled by Corneille since *Cinna* is seen in the way in which Tite translates Auguste's self-declared mastery of himself and of the universe into "Master of the universe without mastery over myself" (407).[16] Like Pauline, Tite expects to find, if not happiness, at least a certain tranquillity in marrying Domitie and, like so many heroes before him, he thinks that his decision will be most secure if he pushes Bérénice into Domitian's arms, thus closing the doors of escape; but his resolve weakens in the presence of the woman he loves. He wants to love Domitie and considers his will sufficient to make him "in spite of love, master of appearances," hoping that constraint turns to habit (950–51), but his will is impotent: while he speaks as emperor, he cannot help but feel as a lover.

Not too surprisingly the split between the private and the public being is once again best illustrated by two women, and once again the duality is present externally, in the contrast between the rivals, and as an internal struggle within each human heart.

Domitie considers the art of truly loving a ridiculous honor which will not charm her away from her worthier ambitions (217–22), and intends to control her heart for the sake of her glory. She loves not Tite but his throne, and when he questions her as to her true feelings she shuts out his questions as irrelevant, considering that a "truly noble heart is satisfied with appearances" (1557). Compounding this undesirable trait is Domitie's pettiness. Her attitude is less one of genuine jealousy than of wounded pride. Though she does not love Tite, she expects him to love her, and reacts with blistering tirades whenever he shows any other sentiment. By the same token, though she represses her love for Domitian, she cannot stand the thought of losing him to Bérénice.

Her most damning trait, however, is that her search for glory is a selfish one, one in which glory is mistakenly identified with pure power. Although she feels the pangs of love, and although her self-mastery is quite painful (63–152), she also feels that to love less than an emperor is to love against her interests (230). As Domitian finds out soon enough, she considers and loves only herself (276). As a result she must, like Honorie before her, rely on those who surround her to achieve her goals in the political smelter that is Rome. It is in this context that she asks Domitian for constant proof of his love, and if he will not sacrifice his love to her desires—"If you love me, my lord, you must save my glory" (1187)—if she cannot be empress, "I will belong to whoever avenges me" (1204). Joining Chimène, Emilie, and a whole line of women willing to prostitute themselves for the sake of a goal they cannot reach on their own, Domitie once more proves the sterility of that self-seeking concept of glory.

Bérénice seeks a different type of glory altogether, and the difference is once again brought out during the direct confrontations (III, 2 and 3). Bérénice is not devoid of consideration for power (1131–32), but she has no problem relegating these feelings, just as she eventually surmounts her wounded pride and forgives her rival to the point where she suggests that Tite marry Domitie. Bérénice and Domitie live in such different worlds, with such different values, that they do not even understand each other. Even though Domitie is capable of love she neither understands nor believes in Bérénice's purer love (1528–46). Bérénice not only loves without regard for politics, but she is impatient with whoever considers them (927–28) and, secure in her love, she demands only that Tite love her in return. Although Rome adopts her she refuses to endanger either love or lover. There is no question here of knowing which of the two—the heroic or the feminine—wins out. In her, the two are one. Her very words prove it, and the woman who asks her lover to act so that they will be loved forever (1702) and who maintains that a true love never exposes the beloved (1712) shows readily that she can give a lesson in *amour généreux* to the noble Tite. If Tite is, "in spite of love, . . . master of things eternal" (950), Bérénice masters them through her love. Her declaration that it is because of her love that she tears herself away from him (1731) is what forces him to acknowledge the lesson (1739) and announce his own self-sacrifice to that supreme love.

Love triumphs, then, as it did in *Le Cid*, at the cost of intense human sacrifice, and, as in that early play, it is a rational love, not some senseless passion, Bérénice's final decision having been dictated by reason (1726) in spite of Tite, and in spite of herself. Pertharite had wanted to find happiness at all costs. Bérénice saves love by tearing herself away from happiness. Content with Tite's love (1714) she is mistress of herself and of the situation and thus is in a position to give to Domitie that which the Roman could not attain by herself. That is the supreme irony: Domitie, who subjugated everything to her pride, must now accept everything (love, lover, eventually the throne) from the hands of a rival who, the victim of circumstances, has snatched victory from the jaws of defeat by her ultimate transcendence of things temporal.

IX   *Pulchérie* [17]

Racine having become the more or less official author of the Bourgogne troupe, and Molière's troupe having failed Corneille in its production of *Tite et Bérénice*, the old dramatist decided to give his next play to the nearly defunct Marais company. In the dedicatory letter, Corneille told the reader that the public once again had learned the path to a place where theater was thought dead and where, in spite of obscure actors, his play had had quite a success. He ended the letter with the hope that the reading public would give *Pulchérie* the same reception. Little did he know how accurate this prediction was to be: *Pulchérie*'s popularity on stage was very short-lived, and its printing history indicates an analogous fate with the readers.

Stubbornly refusing to yield to the notions of the times, Corneille again used the appellation "heroic comedy" to describe a play in which neither life nor state are at stake, an unfortunate obstinacy considering the content of the play. Like *Tite et Bérénice, Pulchérie* deals with a person in love elevated to a throne and therefore unable to simultaneously do full justice to both love and duty. The basic difference is that this time it is the ruler who breaks the bonds of love, isolating herself and creating a truly tragic situation.

Pulchérie, granddaughter of Theodosius, and Léon, a young nobleman, are in love. Martian, an old minister, is well aware of his age yet loves Pulchérie, while his daughter Justine loves Léon. The emperor having died, Pulchérie suggests Léon as his successor in the hope of then marrying him. When she is elected instead, she asks the senate to select Léon as her husband. The senate, refusing that task, asks her to choose her own mate, and Pulchérie now feels obligated to reject Léon: loving him as she does, she might allow him to become her master, a situation acceptable neither to her nor to the senate whose more powerful members consider Léon too young and untried. To keep intact both her love and her sense of duty, Pulchérie gives her hand—but only her hand—to Martian, and Léon to Justine, with the understanding that Léon will be the next emperor.

As can be seen from the above, the plot is very simple. Gone are the days of intricate meanderings and suspenseful ups and downs of fortune. There are only six characters: the four principals; Léon's sister Irène; and her lover Aspar, an ambitious rival for the throne. The entire play could be synopsized in a single sentence: Pulchérie, having become empress, can no longer marry the man she loves and therefore contracts a *mariage blanc* with another. Echoing Tite's "I have the eyes of an emperor, and no longer those of Tite" (495), Pulchérie capsulizes the entire action in a magnificent line: "I am empress, and I was Pulchérie" (754). *Pulchérie,* then, is not a play of interactions and relationships but of a single traumatic experience that cannot be shared. From the opening line—"I love you Léon, and do not hide the fact"—Pulchérie tries to establish relationships which as empress she will no longer find viable.

Of all the heroines of the older Corneille, Pulchérie is the loneliest and the most isolated. Victim of her sense of duty, she is surrounded by people unable to understand her. But such a facile characterization hides a very complex situation. "In the political tetralogy one loved only whom one was born to love and destiny rarely made a mistake in the case of the central characters of the piece." [18] Pulchérie is not so fortunate. Although she loves Léon with a love that will go to the grave and beyond (847–54), she will not allow that feeling to rule her (759) once her duty lies in another direction. Although her feelings for Léon are predicated on virtue and reason (10), with the changing situation marriage has even greater goals (80). "Love moans in vain under the weight of severe duty" (85). Thus, like the Infante, Pulchérie will have to give up the lover she cannot have herself lest she forget her duty to herself and to her glory: "I fear him, I fear myself, if he does not commit his heart" (867). Her decision is as obvious as was the Infante's, but she is far less decisive. Her love is too strong to be denied easily. Even when prodded to rush her decision she hesitates, reluctant to commit herself. Her decision is all the more difficult in that she is surrounded by human beings, not heroes, by lovers ready to sacrifice themselves to their love, and such tendencies are contagious. Whereas the Infante reentered a generous world via her sacrifice, Pulchérie estranges herself from those who surround her by hers. Sensing this, her decision comes only at the end of an almost unbearable struggle between the human and the heroic which is the very stuff this play is made of. Although the problem is presented early enough, Pulchérie has not yet made up her mind in the third act (878–79), and by the fourth act she still maintains that she has not made an irrevocable gift (1174).

To better understand the nature of the relationships between Pulchérie on the one hand and the rest of the characters on the other, one has but to look at the dramatis personae: no confidants, just six characters, four of which are able to confide in a relative on stage (Martian and his daughter Justine, Irène and her brother Léon). Aspar, a despicable Machiavellian, and Pulchérie occupy the lonely poles. In between gravitate these four human beings that deserve perhaps a closer look. These are not petty characters such as the ones seen gravitating around Médée, and they are on the whole very sincere, though some questions might be raised concerning Irène.

Of the four, Martian is perhaps the most interesting. Fully aware of his age and the ridicule of his passion, he has kept his love of Pulchérie quiet. Sensing his rivals better suited than he, he suffers all the pangs of jealousy imaginable. Despite this he loves selflessly because, as he claims, "Love attaches itself to the beloved against itself" (425–26). The advice he gives to his daughter is in the same vein: "True love has no self-interest" (719), and he suggests that the two work against their own interests and for those of the ones they love.

Irène also loves unselfishly. Aware of Aspar's lack of feelings for her, she enjoys teasing him. When, after two years of waiting, she finds herself abandoned by him, she tries to put on a "heroic face," and "under a beautiful exterior, devour her sorrow" (1107–12), but the mask is ineffective and she soon again confesses the supremacy of her love: "I love you/ More than myself" (1373–74) she tells Aspar when his Machiavellian schemes endanger his life. "Love is tender and timid, and fears for the beloved" (1375), and her fears are such that she is willing to sacrifice herself and her glory for him: "Disdain me, leave me, but do not destroy yourself" (1384).

Justine and Léon never hesitate; their undivided efforts are in the service of love. Léon seeks the throne only because it is a means of obtaining Pulchérie, and he repeatedly states his willingness to give up all political dreams for the sake of his love.

One thing unites these five principles, and that is a rejection of the values espoused by Aspar. Rebuked by all, his union with Irène is left in abeyance at the end of the play, but not his political future. In their discourses with Aspar, the more generous characters frequently show their contempt with cutting irony, as when Pulchérie calls his feelings for Irène "beautiful love" (1314). At times, this irony lapses into grating black humor, as in the third scene of the fourth act. Having hinted that an insurrection is brewing, Aspar refuses to name its leader. Pulchérie returns the favor and tells him that she has been warned against a personal enemy and then uses Aspar's very words in her refusal to divulge the name of that foe. Black comedy at its most ferocious, its sole purpose here is to mark the gulf that separates Aspar from the others.

Pulchérie's solitude derives from her attempts to unite two tendencies within one heart but not because of some basic and tragic flaw. Trying to be both lover and ruler she must stifle a love that she once declared to be good. Her evolution is a hardening of a posture, a growing estrangement from the humanity she once shared with her protagonists. Léon, totally given over to his love, cannot accept this and, unable to follow Pulchérie in her metamorphosis, leaves her alone in her quest for glory and fulfillment. Like Bérénice, Pulchérie sacrifices her happiness to that glory and, in so doing, saves her love.

Yet ironically, this play does not end with the victory of love. Martian is accepted not as a lover, but as a proven servant of the state. Justine is united with Léon not because of her love, but as a means of assuring his ascent to the throne. Love does not triumph over glory—and it is perhaps for this reason that the play failed, going as it did against the tastes of the times. Rather, the two elements unite, relaxing the tension and dissolving the tragic mood. It is thanks to this synthesis that the play could be construed as deserving the label of "heroic comedy." As has been seen, this synthesis is achieved very slowly and with great difficulty as far as the Cornelian women are concerned. Men, who cannot hide behind the expedient "weakness" of their sex, find it even more difficult; yet, as we shall see, in his last play Corneille tried, and indeed succeeded, in attaining that goal.

X *Suréna*

Eurydice, daughter of the king of Armenia, and Suréna, Parthian general who has helped Orode to regain the throne of Parthia, are in love, even though Eurydice is engaged to Pacorus, son of Orode, and Suréna to Mandane, the king's daughter. To complicate matters Palmis, sister of Suréna, is in love with Pacorus, who once loved her. While Eurydice is willing to sacrifice her love on the altar of duty, Suréna feels that he cannot violate his vow to Eurydice who, moreover, asks him not to marry Mandane. Suspecting that he has a rival, Pacorus tries in vain to find out his identity, and is joined in that quest by his politically motivated father. As Sillace, the Machiavellian adviser, tells Orode, a man as powerful as Suréna must be killed or brought into the family (729–30). When Suréna refuses to marry Mandane, the King suspects the truth and turns Sillace's suggestion into an ultimatum. Before such a threat Palmis tries to save her brother by asking Eurydice to yield, but in vain. In a last attempt the King demands one of the two marriages, but there is again a dual rejection, Eurydice refusing to marry Pacorus while Suréna is in danger. From then on the outcome is set, no longer depending on the two lovers who can only wait for the inevitable:

the death of Suréna by order of the King, followed by the death of Eurydice of a broken heart.

Despite the length of the above, *Suréna* is a very compact, straightforward play, with a simple and realistic intrigue and a truly tragic ending. In the entire play there are only eighteen scenes and seven people; the action is uninterrupted by the usual *récits,* nothing detracting from the steady increase in dramatic tension. Technically, there are two *récits,* one by Eurydice to introduce the play's a priori, one of five lines by her lady-in-waiting to tell us of Suréna's death. To fully sense the effectiveness and the dramatic correctness of these five lines it is important to keep them in context, for they are far more than a matter of fact bow to theatrical conventions and to public taste. As the death of Suréna becomes more and more certain, the tension rises to fever pitch. When Suréna exits, Palmis tries one last effort to convince Eurydice of the necessity to give her lover to her rival, and she succeeds. As the audience feels the effect of this surrender, Ormène enters and in just a few words announces that it is all over. After that snapping of the dramatic tension, extended verbiage, whatever its mood might be, would be terribly anticlimactic. As it is, the *récit* merely aids in the preparation for the culmination of the tragedy. The death of Eurydice on stage, though a violation of all the rules of classical dramaturgy, is thus made natural and perhaps even a necessity.

Suréna, far from being an anomaly, is a most Cornelian play in many ways. It is, first and foremost, a play in which the Machiavellian and the generous must fight it out, and in which integrity is sacrificed to reasons of state or, better perhaps, to the vanity of insecure mediocrities. The central act, Act III, belongs to Orode who is present throughout it, and the central scene of that act is the confrontation Orode-Suréna. Still, it cannot be denied that the greatness of the play lies not in that it rehashed old verities, but in that it gave them a new twist. To better see the nature of that innovation it is imperative to first take a closer look at some of the main characters.

Though the plot obviously revolves around Suréna, the major role is undoubtedly that of Eurydice, who is absent from stage during only six scenes.[19] As in so many previous cases, her traits are best revealed if contrasted with those of the second female lead, Palmis, for it is within that contrast that Corneille gives us his ultimate try at defining *l'éternel féminin*.

As revealed in some of the most touching love duets in all of Corneille, Eurydice is proud yet extremely gentle. A more tender Infante, she loves a man whose worth defies the normal dynastic order of things and who is above "a king who is only king" (64). Yet, while Suréna may be a king-maker like Rodrigue (60) and if his hand is worth more to Eurydice than a diadem (233), he is nonetheless not a king and therefore unworthy of a love that Eurydice reveals to all, even to Suréna to whom she declares her willingness to "ever love, ever suffer, ever die" (268), a line that Suréna will echo in closing one of the greatest love duets of all (348). However egotistical she may show herself to be at times, Eurydice is able to completely identify with the man she loves. When asked to name her lover, she identifies him as the man worthiest of her that she has ever known (540).

Eurydice is one of the most open and frank of all Cornelian heroines. To Pacorus she offers her hand without her heart because "my heart has made no treaty with you" (504). Though she promises to do her best to move her heart for him, she confesses that these efforts may be in vain (507). Such frankness has distinct drawbacks: when Pacorus finally forces her to admit her love for another, she rescinds her promise to marry him and demands that he first make her forget her love for Suréna and make her love him (549–64).

In fact, all the lovers in *Suréna* are remarkably frank. Palmis scolds Pacorus for forsaking her and promises to forgive him if he can truly say that duty forced him to do it. When he openly admits that love compelled him, she reacts only by confessing that it a really makes no difference, since she cannot bring herself to hate him (674).

Both women realize that the presence of the beloved is a painful necessity, though the reasons are not quite the same. Eurydice in love and painfully torn seems at times to wallow in that pain, but that is because she sees in it a further proof of her love. Palmis, on the other hand, wants to be near "the ingrate that kills [her]" (1001) because she will thus see him "worried, alarmed by the thought of an unknown rival . . . become her victim" (1007–10). In other words, she wants to be with him to await the moment when he will regret her (1020). Yet it is Palmis, seemingly here most selfish and tenacious, who most readily reveals her tenderness at the crucial moment. With Suréna's life in danger, Eurydice feigns a lack of concern that brings a quick reproach from Palmis (1097–98). Eurydice explains that her "intrepidity is only an effort of glory" which her tender heart will not believe (1117–19).[20] Tender, yes, but unable to surrender Suréna, though her refusal may cost him his life: "To give the man one adores to the woman one wants to hate,/ What love could ever betray itself to that extent?" (1703–4). Palmis cannot mention all the Cornelian heroines who were able to sacrifice themselves to just such an extent, but her reproach certainly indicates that she could have been of that number herself. Eurydice's love, in Palmis' eyes, is not only "useless" (1725), but since it exists only to cause Suréna's death (1728), it is far from perfect.

Pitted simultaneously against the possessive passion of Pacorus and the Machiavellian fears of Orode, Suréna is only the victim of fate insofar as he has been fated to be a better man than his king, and the man worthiest of Eurydice. In all other respects he lives and dies by resolutely insisting on the survival of his integrity.

Suréna has beaten his King's foes. The King has gotten the rewards; Suréna, the glory. But it is offensive for a king to owe too much to a subject (705–6), and, to remedy the situation, Orode decides to bring Suréna into the family. To do this, he must disregard a love that antedates his problems, and in so negating human values, he commits his first error as a wise ruler. This error leads the King to a crime, both morally and politically, for which the heavens are sure to punish him.[21] Between Orode's marital ultimatum and Suréna's death, there lies the most important decision of the entire play, Suréna's refusal to surrender to the King's orders.

Suréna is not unaware of glory, of posterity, but none of this "cold and vain eternity" (312) is worth one moment of genuine happiness. Rejection of temporal values had already occurred in *Tite et Bérénice* (1483–86), but never to this extent. "Let everything die with me," Suréna says (301), divorcing once and for all public honors from the concept of generosity. There is much melancholy and tenderness in Suréna, but he is not devoid of strength of character for all that. On the contrary, if he has, when the need arises, enough firmness to tear himself away from the tender trap that is Eurydice (1675), it is because of an inner strength that is at the basis of his formidable decision. Orode and Suréna are, in many ways, like Agésilas and Lysander, only this time the powerful subject considers duty to conscience to be above duty to the King. Limiting the King's power by telling him that "the empire of the hearts is not of your empire" (1310), he refuses to yield to either threats or promises, and insists on remaining his own creature (1347–48). It is beneath this generous soldier's dignity to compromise his conscience just to avoid a tyrant's whimsical order, be it for marriage or death. He will not allow the King over his glory, only over his life (1380), and if the King therefore wants him dead, then his death is inevitable (1614).

This leads us to the crucial matter of his rejection of Mandane. As Suréna so clearly sees, it is not his refusal to marry her that seals his fate, nor is it his love for Eurydice. His real "crime" is to have a greater reputation and more virtue than the King (1509–14). Under the circumstances, why should he prostitute himself needlessly? In that sense, his love and generosity go hand in hand, both dictating the rejection of the compromises offered. As André Stegmann has said, "Thus Suréna, first a lover, finds in his lover's duty a faithfulness to himself that transcends love." [22] As a "just choice" had been the cause of the death of Sertorius (1680), so now an equally lucid choice will be the death of Suréna, a death foreseen by Eurydice (1122) who cannot prevent it (1135–36), although she is fully aware of the consequences.

When Eurydice and Suréna, joined by their refusal to yield to contingencies as much as by their love, find in this ultimate reconciliation of love and generosity an escape from the Sisyphean hell to which their dramatic predecessors were condemned, Corneille has earned the right to close the book of his dramatic career. It is therefore to this great moment in French dramatic literature that I would like to devote the last few paragraphs of this chapter.

In this play of obvious political clashes, the tension is strangely interiorized, and no deus ex machina can solve that problem. Temporal glory, tyrant over human emotions, is opposed by love, the destroyer of the heroic essence. If one word had to be chosen as omnipresent, it would have to be *soupirs*—sighs—and Eurydice constantly speaks of her "enslaved heart." But that is not the main problem. We are dealing here with a group of voluntarily deaf people; everyone understands everyone else but refuses to act according to that comprehension.[23] They are all playing a rigidly codified game whose basic tenets they know, yet disregard. To give but one example: Pacorus, jealously and unreasonably demands the heart as well as the hand of his political betrothed. This Eurydice cannot grant him, and, when he forces the issue, Eurydice must retract even her original willingness to go through the political union and insist in turn on the impossible, since by revealing her failing, Pacorus has made the removal of that flaw a prerequisite of any further agreement.

This then is the mood that prevails at the court of King Orode. But in this infernal milieu, a couple has found a way to escape. Bérénice, by her sacrifice to love (859–71), had made a hero of Tite in Judea, had made him worthy of becoming emperor. Their love dated from that time and land foreign to the Rome in which the action of the play takes place. *Suréna* is, in that sense, a variation on an old theme, in that Suréna and Eurydice fell in love in Armenia while Suréna was winning his laurels. It is this relationship that antedates the action of the play and which they jealously guard against defiling intruders.

In that private world, from which even Palmis is excluded, Suréna and Eurydice share the fruits of their lucidity. Doomed by it to forever "love, suffer, and die," they respond by wrenching themselves away from all the impasses, the temporal, the repetitive becoming. That last effort is nothing less than a liberating— how ironically true is Suréna's belated "I am free" (1667)—élan to authenticity, and nothing consecrates it more than Eurydice's last words (1732, 1734), a sublime cry of love that shows that Palmis' more obvious sacrifices were perhaps not of the highest order. In a truly Pascalian sense (since the victims know why they die, and the universe that crushes them does not), the victims become the victors.

As André Stegmann states in his introduction to *Suréna*, "it is with this anti-Machiavellian profession of faith that Corneille closes his dramatic career. To this central theme, he adds an interesting counterpoint which transcends the political problem and gives the element of duration to the heretofore temporal notion of glory. To that 'cold and vain eternity' he opposes an inner freedom, the only force and refuge against all the vicissitudes of fate. It is this freedom which allows the hero to die not only justified, but without regrets." [24] This is the solution that the early heroes of Corneille, the Rodrigues, the Horaces, had been seeking. It is the ultimate solution that only the last ones found.

CHAPTER 6

Conclusion

EVEN today, it is not too unusual, in France and abroad, for critics to view Corneille through lenses fogged by too close a contact with the great political tetralogy (*Le Cid, Horace, Cinna, Polyeucte*). The result is that these plays then become the standards of what is "Cornelian" or not, and any evolutionary tendency of the author—be it for better or for worse—becomes a deviation from set norms. One recent critic, for instance, asserted that outside of a small handful of plays there were no Cornelian heroes in the works of Corneille. Would it be sillier to suggest that there are no more Frenchmen in France because no one acts like Charles Boyer anymore? Corneille, like any other writer worth his salt and blessed with so many productive years, managed to evolve without changing his basic principles. To abstract criteria from one stage of that evolution and apply them to later stages, judging the plays of these by whether or not they conform, is to prejudice oneself against, and even blind oneself to, any of the positive changes that the author wrought in his system. I hope that in the preceding chapters I have not only avoided that pitfall, but have also shown, within the limitations of this brief study, some of the major aspects of that system and the changes that Corneille evolved as the years went by.

Few generalizations can be made about this long career, yet some are not entirely out of order. While Corneille was ever in search of renewal, while his maturation process and his growing weariness are easily discerned, there are some invariables, so traceable as to constitute *leitmotifs*.

The Cornelian hero, urged by a latent or overt generous essence on a path to the absolute, is everywhere confronted by mediocrities or social forces mired in the relative values of expediency. Their task is hopeless, but as Camus put it in the *Myth of Sisyphus,* lack of hope has nothing to do with despair, and they invariably strive to stay on their initial course. Thus, Chimène will ever do her best to avenge her father while hoping to fail (992–94), and Suréna will take care of his *gloire* regardless of what his king will do (1380), though some will view their Sisyphian condemnation with far less alacrity than others. In that sense the comedies should be viewed not as of a different coin from the tragedies, but as the other side of the same coin. The readiness with which Dorante can be fraudulent in his love affairs and the lessons in *amour généreux* given by Rodrigue or Bérénice are surely manifestations of a single concern. In fact, Dorante and Rodrigue can be defined in toto by their attitudes toward love: Dorante believes that fraud is legitimate, Rodrigue clearly sees that there is but one honor.

Another constant—though not as discernible in the first three plays of the tetralogy and in *Suréna*—is Corneille's habit of emphasizing the gulf that exists between the two above-mentioned worlds by juxtaposing them, creating a grating black humor that some critics have deplored, but which splendidly shows off the solitude of the hero. Médée alone is tragic among comic figures and never is this more obvious than when she has to resort to irony or sarcasm; Félix's willingness to profit by Polyeucte's death gives rise to some hollow laughter that defines the line of demarcation between the two men better than any grandiloquent tirade could have done. The buffoonery of the mediocrities may at times be painful, but who ever suggested that the laughter in *King Lear* was salutary or sane? It takes an old lecher posturing as a monarch, a "queen" worried about a dress, to make us fully participate in the superiority, the isolation, the estrangement, and even the nausea of the tragic hero. When a Félix becomes aware of his inferiority, when a Suréna realizes that his doom is sealed precisely because his king has discovered in himself an inferiority that he can only resent, Corneille may be mixing tones, but to create a uniquely and purely tragic atmosphere.

From *Mélite* to *Suréna* there are, in spite of these constants, some steady progressions. The youthful heroes of the earlier plays are exuberant and prone to instinctive reactions such as the one Rodrigue has to his father's challenge. Of course, Rodrigue's instinct is of necessity closely tied to his generous essence, and so it is, if the term may be forgiven, a reasonable one. All of Corneille's heroes are reasonable, but Rodrigue is not always able to reason. Suréna is not only reasonable but reasoning. As a result, he is not only more of an *honnête homme*, an urbane gentleman, he is also more sympathetic and, above all, more human. There are times—and this is particularly true in political plays such as *Othon*—when Corneille's characters reason too much. In *Horace* and *Cinna* the presence of dialectic scenes is permissible, even salutary, but *Othon* is excessively cerebral. Its persistent, minute analyses of the human mind challenge the intellectual reader, but by flying in the face of trends toward the pathetic it failed to attract a theater audience in the seventeenth century, and will always fail to do so. Such plays are nevertheless not without appeal. Turenne, marshal of Louis XIV, having seen *Sertorius*, was so struck by the realism of the political analyses, particularly those dealing with civil war, that he is said to have exclaimed, "Where did Corneille learn the art of war?" Napoleon, because of such plays, saw in Corneille the only French poet who understood politics. Not everyone may share Turenne's or Napoleon's interests, but however unstageworthy some of these plays may be, they should be read if only for the light that they shed on the evolution of Corneille's dramatic canon.

There is another—and more important—evolution in the Cornelian hero. Readers of *Suréna*, who previously knew Corneille only from the early plays, are struck by the tired, hesitating, regretful hero, and see the play as an exceptional departure from Cornelian standards. One has but to look at the heroes (and even better, at the heroines) of the plays of the middle period to see the fallacy of that first impression.[1] From beginning to end, Corneille's tragic heroines are aware of their obligations to themselves and to their reputation. Many, particularly in the earlier plays, find the path to fulfillment in the assumption of a masculine mystique which can only frustrate them and make true happiness impossible. As the author grew older he created an ever increasing number of heroines who sought a different path. If, in *Rodogune*, Cléopatre reminds us of Lady Macbeth's "unsex me," Ildione, in *Attila*, violates her *gloire* for the sake of her "natural sweetness" (1448), and Palmis, in *Suréna*, uses the world *gloire* only once— and that in connection with love. In these later plays those heroines seeking their fulfillment in the "glorious" manner find their path more and more difficult, not because of outside barriers, but because of a growing awareness of their true nature and because of hearts that will not be stilled. Time and time again it is in the assumption of this true nature that these heroines attain a level far above that reached by the slaves of the Roman grandeur so readily associated with the earlier plays.

Very early in his career Corneille created works of art in which admiration for heroic stature was of paramount importance. With *Nicomède* that admiration became the sole spring, excluding those feelings normally considered the sine qua non of tragedy. Yet, as of *La Toison d'or* (1982–85), one senses a growing pessimism in the author and in those of his heroes tired of the treadmill of temporal causes. *Suréna* is therefore not an anomaly; it is the successful end of a long quest. When, during the last years of his productive life, Corneille was stubbornly rejecting the dictates of fashion and advice of those critics who told him to retire, he was groping for an answer to a question he had repeatedly posed since *Médée*. With *Suréna*, a masterpiece in every sense of the word, he gave his answer, one that was ignored for nearly three centuries and which only in the last few decades has been recognized for what it is: a great work of art that summarizes the intellectual and creative travail of a lifetime.

Notes and References

Chapter One

1. *Œuvres* (Paris: Hachette, 1862–68), X, 64–72, 74–78. Except for the early comedies, all references pertaining to the works of Corneille will be to this edition prepared by Ch. Marty-Laveaux. References to plays will be by means of line numbers in parentheses.

2. Many studies have centered around this touchy union. The best of these remain the book by L. Batiffol, *Richelieu et Corneille* (Paris: Calmann-Lévy, 1936), and articles by Sister M. Amelia Klenke and H. C. Lancaster in *PMLA* 64 (1949), 724–45; 65 (1950), 322–28.

3. *L'héroïsme cornélien* (Paris: Colin, 1968), I, 49.

4. For a fuller treatment of this idea, see *ibid.*, I, 86–87.

5. *Ibid.*, I, 129.

6. *Corneille* (Paris: Fayard, 1961), p. 199.

7. Louise d'Orléans, duchess of Montpensier, commonly called La Grande Mademoiselle, took an active part in the Fronde and, during the battle of the Faubourg Saint-Antoine, personally supervised the shelling of the royal troops. Paul de Gondi, later Cardinal de Retz, one of the leaders of the resistance, was considered by most as little more than an adventurer and intriguer.

8. *Corneille,* p. 243.

9. In the *Examen,* written in 1660, he was to make a much better case for the play, pointing out its many strong points.

10. These critical writings can be of great help to the student of Corneille, but they must be used with great care, for the mature Corneille, in discussing the plays of his youth, not only failed to recapture their spirit but purposefully misrepresented them to make them more acceptable to the new breed of literati. The same must be said of the corrections he made: whether they improved the plays is debatable at best; that they radically altered them, masking the original tone, is not.

11. Robert Brasillach, *Corneille,* p. 229.

12. *Ibid.,* p. 235.

13. Interestingly enough, 1656 is also the date of the biggest dramatic success of the century, that of his brother Thomas' *Timocrate.*

14. André Stegmann, *L'héroïsme,* I, 173.

15. *"Contre le goût du temps"* is how he himself qualified the main character of *Pulchérie* in its prefatory letter, but in that same letter he proudly defied the "stubbornness of the century."

16. See especially lines 1379–80 and 1509–26.

17. *Œuvres*, X, 313.

18. *L'œil vivant* (Paris: Gallimard, 1961), p. 18.

19. *Œuvres* (Paris: Seuil, 1962), 413–14.

Chapter Two

1. For a thorough analysis of this phenomenon, see Jean Starobinski, *L'œil vivant*, p. 31.

2. Robert J. Nelson, *Corneille. His Heroes and Their Worlds* (Philadelphia: University of Pennsylvania Press, 1963), p. 27.

3. *Histoire de la littérature française au XVIIe siècle* (Paris: Del Duca, 1962), I, 484.

4. See Act II, scene 2, for instance.

5. For a detailed analysis of these changes, see L. Rivaille, *P. Corneille, correcteur de ses premières œuvres* (1632–44) (Paris: Boivin, 1936).

6. If further testimony were required, one might point to direct references to *Mélite* (955–58), a ploy Corneille was to use again several times in later plays.

7. *Corneille*, p. 42.

8. "The Hero in Corneille's Early Comedies," *PMLA* 78 (June, 1963), 198.

9. Most dictionaries translate *suivante* as "waiting-maid," but a fuller understanding of the term—and of the heroine of this play—will be obtained if one keeps in mind that *suivantes* were ladies or girls of good families, often equal in birth and education to their mistresses, but forced by poverty to perform the tasks of attendants.

10. *Corneille*, p. 52.

11. "The Hero," p. 199.

12. Such a parody will readily be apparent—this time legitimately as far as chronology is concerned—in a later play, *Le Menteur*.

13. *Le sentiment de l'amour dans l'œuvre de Pierre Corneille* (Paris: Gallimard, 1948), p. 111.

14. Between *La Place Royale* and *Médée*, Corneille collaborated on the composition of the *Comédie des Tuileries* by the "Five Authors." His contribution, limited to the third act for which he had been handed a sketch to retouch and fill out, cannot be pinpointed. It is therefore impossible to properly assess its importance in the development of the Cornelian canon. Furthermore, the merits of that act, like those of the rest of the play, make it all too easy to omit the play from discussion altogether.

15. "The Captive Audience in *L'Illusion comique,*" *MLN* 81 (1966), 343.

Chapter Three

1. (New York: Dell, 1963), pp. 24–25.

2. "A Minimal Definition of Seventeenth-Century Tragedy," *FS* 10 (1956), 305.

3. For a fuller examination of this see Henri Gouhier, "Tragique et transcendance," in *Le théâtre tragique,* ed. J. Jacquot (Paris: CNRS, 1962), p. 479.

4. *L'œil vivant,* p. 18.

5. Robert J. Nelson, *Corneille,* pp. 20–21.

6. For a more thorough discussion of the above points, see my monograph, *The Strangers: The Tragic World of Tristan L'Hermite* (Gainesville: University of Florida Press, 1966), pp. 1–21, and my article, "Hommes et masques cornéliens," *FR* 44 (February, 1971), 523–34.

7. In tone, Médée has a few momentary lapses which might easily be interpreted as attempts on her part to communicate with the creatures of Jason's world.

8. *Corneille* (Paris: L'Arche, 1957), p. 40.

9. The legitimacy of this position can be argued by referring to the Hamlets and Orestes of literature and history.

10. A. Donald Sellstrom, "The Rome of Corneille's Infante," *FR* 39 (November, 1965), 240.

11. *La littérature de l'âge baroque en France* (Paris: Corti, 1965), p. 213.

12. *Corneille,* p. 87.

13. It should be remembered that *Horace* was dedicated to Richelieu!

14. During the seventeenth century some people called the play *Les Horaces.* It might be well to keep in mind that Corneille did not.

15. Robert Brasillach, *Corneille,* p. 129.

16. Théodore, the heroine of Corneille's play by that name, put it quite simply: "Whover chooses, consents, and to consent is cowardly and shameful" (773–74).

17. Corneille was not averse to having characters make such shaking suggestions, as we shall see in later plays, particularly in *Rodogune.*

18. "The Metaphor of Origins in *Horace,*" *FR* 40 (November, 1966), 244.

19. *L'héroïsme,* II, 583.

20. Maurice Descotes, *Les grands rôles du théâtre de Corneille* (Paris: PUF, 1966), p. 163.

21. Some critics consider that another autobiographic statement whereby the newly married Corneille was announcing the end of an era.

22. *Polyeucte, étude et analyse* (Paris: Mellottée, 1932), pp. 181–82.

23. Interestingly enough, while Rodrigue tries to teach a lesson to his father, Pauline can only agree to be once more "victim of his orders" (364). And yet, in the final analysis, Félix is saved by his daughter while Rodrigue cannot bring his father into his world.

24. *Polyeucte*, pp. 188–92.

25. Michel Beaujour, "*Polyeucte* et la monarchie de droit divin," *FR* 36 (April, 1963), 443–49.

26. *L'héroïsme*, II, 463.

Chapter Four

1. The word is absent from the play but will reappear in *La Suite du Menteur*.

2. As will be seen later, the *comédie héroïque* is a radically different kind of play.

3. *Corneille* (New York: St. Martin's Press, 1963), pp. 281–82.

4. *Sentiment*, pp. 224–25. It is however impossible to follow Octave Nadal in some of his reasoning, which makes him view Antiochus and Séleucus as children and Rodogune as "*mûre*," that is, ripe. Whatever the two men may be, they are not mere "little princes" in a "love novel," fighting over a woman that vaguely resembles a mother figure (pp. 225, 230, 238).

5. See *Théodore*, line 1156.

6. *Werke* (Munich: Hanser, 1954), I, 48.

7. *Corneille*, p. 146.

8. André Stegmann, *L'héroïsme*, II, 601.

9. *Ibid.*, II, 464.

10. P. J. Yarrow, *Corneille*, p. 116.

11. André Stegmann, *L'héroïsme*, II, 595–96.

12. *Sentiment*, p. 218.

13. *Œuvres*, V, 146.

14. *Histoire*, II, 374–75.

15. André Stegmann, *L'héroïsme*, II, 467.

16. *Ibid.*, II, 605.

17. Many critics have examined the question quite closely, and while there is no proof, it is easy to see why most of them believe that either Mazarin or the queen-mother was that "illustrious voice" that refused to applaud the dramatization of their plight.

18. Robert J. Nelson, *Corneille*, p. 170.

19. The basic flaw of *Don Sanche* is not new to the careful reader of Corneille who must have noticed this author's difficulty with always having a single action smoothly stretched out over five acts. The basic premises of the play are posited quite early, and Corneille then pads the interval between the exposition and the resolution with intricate dialogues on the subtleties of glory, honor, and precious love that may have delighted the salon habitués but leave the modern reader quite cold.

20. Hoping to make a strong impression in his debut before the king, Molière chose *Nicomède* as the best possible vehicle. I have refrained from concentrating on stylistic matters since these would invariably depend on a grasp of the French language which the average reader might not have, but a few words here are appropriate. There can be no doubt that some of this popularity was due to certain timely allusions, that much of it must be credited to the overall qualities of the play. But how many contemporaries could have remained untouched by a play written with a verve they had not sensed since *Le Cid*? How many of them could fail to admire the daring virtuosity of an author who constantly allowed the irony of the hero to verge on comedy, relying on the importance of the historic moment and moral elevation of the protagonist to maintain the tragic mode?

21. What some critics refer to as the "voice of blood" is here but a low whisper which needs a nearly magic ring to be heard.

22. More specific links are particular relationships, such as the one between ruthless stepmother and spineless father, or especially successful scenes that recall analogous ones in previous plays. For example, obviously inspired by the success of the great confrontation between Marcelle and Théodore (II, 4), Corneille pits Nicomède against Arsinoë in stichomythic duels of transparent innuendos (I, 3, for instance) that leave the audience breathless.

23. *Sentiment*, p. 130.

24. It must be remembered that *Nicomède* is not a love story. It is true that the titular hero, given a choice between the throne and Laodice, opts for the latter, but this is a gratuitous decision, since he cannot be king while his father is alive without being a rebel, and that he "will never be" (1782). Love as the mainspring of a Cornelian tragedy has yet to appear.

25. Nicomède had preferred Laodice to a throne, but I must insist again on the notion that his choice had been of a different nature since he had no right to that throne as long as his father lived.

26. Serge Doubrovsky, *Corneille et la dialectique du héros* (Paris: Gallimard, 1963), p. 333.

27. This, by the way, presents another problem, for in so doing does the hero not condemn himself to an even more desolate solitude?

It is to the solution of this new problem that Corneille was to address his last plays.

28. Throughout the play, absurd propositions forever take the place of declarations of love: Grimoald will crown Rodélinde's son if she marries him, or kill him if she does not; Rodélinde will marry Grimoald if he kills her son; and Pertharite, upon his arrival, wants to "buy" Rodélinde by relinquishing his throne.

29. *L'héroïsme,* II, 615.

Chapter Five

1. *Sentiment,* p. 53.

2. André Stegmann, *L'héroïsme,* II, 361–62.

3. *Ibid.,* II, 620.

4. "The Greatest Roman of Them All: Corneille's Sertorius," *Esprit Créateur* 4 (Fall, 1964), 166.

5. *Ibid.,* p. 167.

6. Meaningless since she will die without issue, leaving the throne to Rome after her death (1900). As for Perpenna, "by bringing to a head all the evils of division and divorce, [he] must play the part of scapegoat, while Pompey, who merely by proscrastination has at last become the master of his own destiny, can readily take the place of a much greater Roman than himself at the very moment when he replaces an evil dictator" (Judd Hubert, p. 165).

7. As Sartre points out in *Huis clos,* all deaths are always too soon.

8. *L'héroïsme,* II, 374.

9. It is well to keep in mind that 1664, the year of *Othon,* was also the year of Racine's *La Thébaïde.*

10. Corneille, always eager to vary old themes, reversed the situation found elsewhere. This time, of the two women, it is the tender one that is loved and the prouder one that is rejected.

11. *L'héroïsme,* II, 533.

12. Not to be confused with modern free verse, the *vers libres* of the seventeenth century are heterometric lines with very varied rhyme schemes.

13. As Honorie asks, what is a king forced to obey? (420).

14. Serge Doubrovsky, *La dialectique,* p. 385.

15. *L'héroïsme,* II, 634–35.

16. Since *Cinna,* Corneille has also read La Rochefoucauld—a reading already apparent in *Othon*—particularly the sections on *armour-propre,* self-interest, which rules the protagonists. As Albin, Domitian's confidant, states, "self-love is the source of all other love" (279).

17. Between *Tite et Bérénice* and *Pulchérie* Corneille contributed to Molière's *Psyché,* which was premiered in 1671. The songs were written by Quinault to music by Lully. Molière wrote the plot and

did the versification for the first act and the first scene of the second and third acts. In two weeks Corneille did the versification of the unsung part of the rest. *Psyché* contains some of the most fluid poetry created for the lyrical stage of the seventeenth century, and is a gem of its type, a delightful *pièce à machines*. Yet, for all that, it is a joint effort that sheds little light on the Cornelian canon.

18. Robert J. Nelson, *Corneille*, p. 244.

19. Except for two scenes of Act II, all of Act III, and one scene of Act IV, Eurydice is omnipresent.

20. It is interesting that the word *gloire*, though used by nearly everyone in the play, does not always mean the same thing. Orode's concept is that of the warrior, and it is therefore quite logical that he uses it most frequently in referring to Suréna. For Eurydice the word has varied connotations, ranging from pride in love to the "Orodian" sense. Palmis uses *gloire* only twice, once to refer to the usual values which she has rejected and once to describe her pride in her faithful and unwavering love.

21. Without his main support, how long will Orode be able to face a rebellious people aware of his faults (1611–14)?

22. *L'héroïsme*, II, 568.

23. Compounding this difficulty is the general deceit: Pacorus lies to get to the truth; Suréna and Eurydice, to hide it. No one gives the real reasons for what he does or says, and all—Orode, Pacorus, Eurydice, Suréna, and Palmis—make suggestions and excuses that have little connection with truth.

24. Pierre Corneille, *Œuvres* (Paris: Seuil, 1963), p. 799. The full extent of the rejection of Machiavellism can be seen in lines 1637–62, in which Suréna denies not only bad kings, but politics as a whole.

Chapter Six

1. For a fuller discussion of the evolution of the heroines of Corneille, see my article, "*Tendres* and *Généreuses* in the Later Plays of Corneille," in *Renaissance and Other Studies in Honor of William Leon Wiley*, edited by George Bernard Daniel, Jr. (Chapel Hill: The University of North Carolina Press, 1968), pp. 15–30, from which I have borrowed some ideas throughout this study.

Selected Bibliography

I. Background Materials and General Study Aids

A. Bibliographies

CIORANESCU, ALEXANDRE. *Bibliographie de la littérature française du dix-septième siècle*. 3 vols. Paris: CNRS, 1965–66. The most complete of the available bibliographies, very useful in spite of some errors and omissions.

CABEEN, DAVID C., and JULES BRODY. *A Critical Bibliography of French Literature, Volume III: The Seventeenth Century*. Syracuse: Syracuse Univ. Press, 1961. This volume, edited by Nathan Edelman, while far from complete, should be the most useful to the general reader insofar as it judiciously comments on the items selected for inclusion. Sadly out of date, it must be used with Klapp or, better still, with Gravit et al. (see next item).

GRAVIT, FRANCIS W., et al. *Bibliography of French Seventeenth-Century Studies*. Bloomington: Indiana Univ., 1953–68, and Washington: Geo. Washington Univ., 1969 to date. Although there has been a change in the editorship, this annual bibliography, published for the Modern Language Association French Group III, is still commonly called the "Gravit Bibliography." While it is not truly critical, it is carefully annotated and, for the general reader, the most useful supplement to the "Cabeen."

KLAPP, OTTO. *Bibliographie d'histoire littéraire française*. Frankfurt: Klostermann, 1956 to date. Appearing every two years, this is the most complete of the periodic bibliographies, and should be used to complete the standard works.

B. Dictionaries

DUBOIS, J. and R. LAGANE. *Dictionnaire de la langue française classique*. Paris: Belin, 1960. Indispensable, especially for the early comedies which are replete with archaisms.

GRENTE, CARDINAL GEORGES. *Dictionnaire des lettres françaises. Le dix-septième siècle*. Paris: Fayard, 1954. First rate for biographical sketches, with longer articles for selected topics.

C. Literary, Historical, Social, and Political Background

ADAM, ANTOINE. *Histoire de la littérature française au dix-septième siècle.* 5 vols. Paris: Domat, 1948–56. The standard work, well balanced and reliable.

HOWARD, W. D. *The Seventeenth Century.* London: Nelson, 1965. Very learned yet eminently readable book on life and letters as a whole.

LANCASTER, HENRY CARRINGTON. *A History of French Dramatic Literature in the XVIIth Century.* 9 vols. Baltimore: Johns Hopkins Univ. Press, 1929–42. Reprinted in 1952 with corrections, this is a monumental work, an indispensable mine of information.

LEBRUN, F. *Le XVIIᵉ siècle.* Paris: Colin, 1967. Exhaustive and up-to-date interpretation of the culture of the times.

LOUGH, JOHN. *An Introduction to Seventeenth-Century France.* New York: McKay, 1969. Unpretentious. As good an introduction as one could wish for.

YARROW, P. J. *A Literary History of France. Vol. II: The Sevententh Century, 1600–1715.* New York: Barnes and Noble, 1967. Most modern and by far the best available in English.

II. Corneille

A. Bibliographies

COUTON, G. "Etat présent des études cornéliennes." *Information littéraire* 8 (1956), 43–48. Balanced sketch of Corneille criticism, unfortunately, like the other two items, out of date.

LE VERDIER, PIERRE, and EDOUARD PELAY. *Additions à la bibliographie cornélienne.* Paris: Rahir, 1908. Supplement to Picot, using the same method and system.

PICOT, EMILE. *Bibliographie cornélienne.* Paris: Fontaine, 1876. Exhaustive, critical bibliography, well indexed.

PRIMARY SOURCES

Œuvres. Ed. by Charles Mary-Laveaux. 12 Vols. Paris: Hachette, 1862–68. Despite its age, still the standard edition of the works. It is quite satisfactory for all but the early comedies. These were drastically revised by the older Corneille, and only the critical editions listed below use the earlier versions as the basic texts.

Mélite. Ed. by Mario Roques and Marion Lièvre. Geneva: Droz, 1950.

Clitandre. Ed. by R.-L. Wagner. Geneva: Droz, 1949.

La veuve. Ed. by Mario Roques and Marion Lièvre. Geneva: Droz, 1954.

La place royalle. Ed. by J.-Ch. Brunon. Paris: Didier, 1962.

Selected Bibliography

L'illusion comique. Ed. by Robert Garapon. Paris: Didier, 1965.

SECONDARY SOURCES

N. B.: It is impossible to list even a significant fraction of the legion of studies dealing with Corneille. (Cioranescu alone lists over 1200 items.) I have therefore listed here only some of the better recent studies, giving preferance to the more general ones.

BRASILLACH, ROBERT. *Corneille.* Paris: Fayard, 1961. Perhaps over-long but fascinating and quite penetrating.

COUTON, GEORGES. *Corneille.* Paris: Hatier, 1958. First-rate synthesis in every way, though somewhat dry.

————. *Réalisme de Corneille.* Disconnected studies dealing mostly with *Mélite* and *Le Cid,* but shedding much light on Corneille as a whole.

DORCHAIN, AUGUSTE. *Pierre Corneille.* Paris: Garnier, 1918. In spite of its age and chauvinism, this remains one of the most complete studies of Corneille.

DORT, BERNARD. *Pierre Corneille, dramaturge.* Paris: L'Arche, 1957. Systematic analysis that links Corneille with his contemporaries and his times in general.

DOUBROWSKI, SERGE. *Corneille et la dialectique du héros.* Paris: Gallimard, 1965. Most difficult to read but well worth the trouble. Subjectivity of author constantly forces the reader to reassess his notions concerning Corneille.

MAURENS, J. *La tragédie sans tragique: le néo-stoïcisme dans l'œuvre de Pierre Corneille.* Paris: Colin, 1966. Far broader than its title implies, this book admirably shows the rapport between Corneille and the ideas of his days.

MAY, GEORGES. *Tragédie cornélienne, tragédie racinienne.* Urbana: Univ. of Illinois Press, 1948. The first one hundred pages are a detailed examination of the essential dramatic principles of Corneille.

NADAL, OCTAVE. *Le sentiment de l'amour dans l'œuvre de Pierre Corneille.* Paris: Gallimard, 1948. Despite the title, touches on almost every aspect of Cornelian ideology. Absolutely brilliant analyses of the plays. A capital work in every sense.

NELSON, ROBERT J. *Corneille, His Heroes and Their Worlds.* Philadelphia: Univ. of Pennsylvania Press, 1963. While one may quarrel with the categories that are too readily used, the detailed analyses are invariably penetrating and judicious.

———— (ed.). *Corneille and Racine. Parallels and Contrasts.* Englewood Cliffs, N.J.: Prentice-Hall, 1966. A collection of critical writings, many of which are now available only in the best libraries.

STAROBINSKI, JEAN. "Sur Corneille." *Temps modernes* (Nov., 1954), 713–729. [Reproduced as the first chapter of *L'œil vivant* (Paris: Gallimard, 1961).] Keen insight into the Cornelian phenomenon of *éblouissement*.

STEGMANN, ANDRÉ. *L'héroïsme cornélien*. 2 vols. Paris: Colin, 1968. The first volume is perhaps the best intellectual biography of Corneille ever written. The second volume is concerned with Cornelian heroism.

YARROW, P. J. *Corneille*. New York: St. Martin's, 1963. The only modern general study of Corneille done in English. Unfortunately, it is not suitable for the general reader: its highly opinionated statements and arbitrary judgments could mislead any but the expert.

Index

Index

May, Georges, 5, 48
Mazarin, Jules, Cardinal, 19, 21-23, 25, 77, 98, 158
Molière, 11, 26, 27-29, 139, 159, 160
Montdory, 9, 16
Montpensier, Duchess of, (La Grande Mademoiselle), 22, 155

Nadal, Octave, 44, 87, 94, 106, 116, 158
Napoleon, 153
Nelson, Robert, 5, 37, 41, 59, 90, 156, 157, 158, 161
Nietzsche, 60, 90, 106

Ovid, 42

Pascal, Blaise, 50, 85
Péguy, Charles, 58
Pellisson, 24
Pradon, 29

Quinault, Philippe, 11, 99, 130, 160

Racine, Jean, 25, 27-31, 32, 33, 35, 37, 48, 77, 90, 118, 135, 136, 139, 160
Rambouillet, Hôtel de, 19

Retz, Paul de Gondi, Cardinal de, 22, 29, 155
Richelieu, Armand, Cardinal de, 9, 10, 15-19, 20-21, 23, 77, 155, 157
Rivaille, L., 156
Rotrou, Jean de, 16
Rousset, Jean, 59

Saint-Evremond, 27
Sartre, 160
Scudéry, Georges, 10, 17, 19
Séguier, 20
Sellstrom, A. Donald, 157
Seneca, 50, 51, 54
Shakespeare, 56, 60, 64, 152
Sourdéac, Marquis de, 117
Starobinski, Jean, 5, 30, 49, 156
Stegmann, André, 5, 16, 59, 66, 79, 93, 94, 112, 120, 124, 129, 147, 148, 155, 158, 160

Torelli, 98
Tristan L'Hermite, 35
Turenne, 152

Valdor, Jean, 10, 23
Vincent de Paul (Saint), 98

Yarrow, P. J., 5, 87, 158